P9-EMJ-916

200 healthy feasts

hamlyn | **all color cookbook**

200 healthy feasts

An Hachette UK company
www.hachette.co.uk

First published in Great Britain in 2011 by Hamlyn,
a division of Octopus Publishing Group Ltd
Endeavour House, 189 Shaftesbury Avenue
London WC2H 8JY
www.octopusbooksusa.com

Copyright © Octopus Publishing Group Ltd 2011

Distributed in the US by
Hachette Book Group USA
237 Park Avenue
New York NY 10017 USA

Distributed in Canada by
Canadian Manda Group
165 Dufferin Street
Toronto, Ontario, Canada M6K 3H6

Some of the recipes in this book have previously appeared in
other books published by Hamlyn.

ISBN: 978-0-600-62396-0

Printed and bound in China

2 3 4 5 6 7 8 9 10

Standard level spoon measurements are used in all recipes.

Ovens should be preheated to the specified temperature
—if using a fan-assisted oven, follow the manufacturer's
instructions for adjusting the time and the temperature.

The Food and Drug Administration advises that eggs should
not be consumed raw. This book contains some dishes made
with raw or lightly cooked eggs. It is prudent for vulnerable
people, such as pregnant and nursing mothers, invalids, the
elderly, babies, and young children to avoid uncooked or
lightly cooked dishes made with eggs. Once prepared, these
dishes should be kept refrigerated and used promptly.

This book includes dishes made with nuts and nut derivatives.
It is advisable for those with known allergic reactions to
nuts and nut derivatives and those who may be potentially
vulnerable to these allergies to avoid dishes made with nuts
and nut oils. It is also prudent to check the labels of
pre-prepared ingredients for the possible inclusion
of nut derivatives.

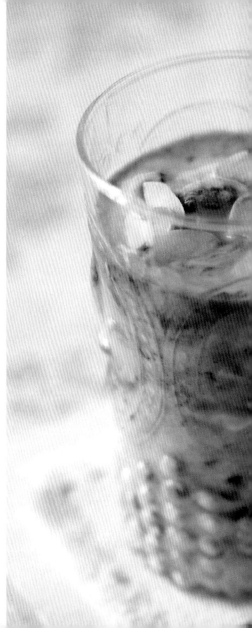

contents

introduction

introduction

If your aim is to eat healthily, but you dread feeling hungry and lacking in energy, then this is the book for you—it is full of delicious, substantial, and nutritious recipes designed to satisfy even the biggest appetites and keep you going until the next meal. This book will show you that "healthy" doesn't have to mean "boring." The great flavors, appearance, and aromas from the recipes it contains will appeal to all your senses, and the energy-boosting ingredients used will help to reduce any craving and your desire to snack while keeping energy levels high. By following the recipes in this book, you will find it easier and

more enjoyable to eat a healthy, well-balanced diet without the feeling that you are being denied all the "good stuff," and this could change the way you eat forever.

reasons to eat healthily

There are so many reasons to keep your body healthy, and the way you eat often has a direct influence on the way you feel. Eating a well-balanced diet with plenty of the essential proteins, vitamins, nutrients, carbohydrates, and essential fats is very important in maintaining good health. It can help control cholesterol, as well going a long way toward avoiding constipation, bad skin, and poor hair condition.

It has also been proven that a healthy diet can help us to avoid serious conditions such as coronary heart disease, strokes, and even some cancers. For example, a diet rich in fiber can reduce the risk of bowel cancer.

The path to general wellbeing through the aid of a healthy diet doesn't usually have to mean a complete overhaul in the way that you eat. More often, it is just a few subtle changes in the way that you think and cook that will leave you reaping the rewards in both the short and long term.

"5 a day"

With the enormous choice and variety available to us today, it's easier than you might think for you and your family to get the recommended minimum of five portions of

fruit and vegetables a day. Almost all fruit and vegetables, and even beans and lentils, count toward one of your "5 a day," whether they come fresh, frozen, dried, or canned.

One adult-sized portion of fruit or vegetable weighs just over 3 oz, or roughly the amount that will fit into the palm of your hand. Even a glass of fruit juice or a smoothie counts, although it's best not to drink more than one of these each day as the sugars they contain can do damage to your teeth in the long term.

Eating at least five portions of fruit and vegetables each day really will improve your health. Consuming your "5 a day" can be achieved on any budget, no matter how busy your lifestyle. It just takes a little planning and effort.

the GI

GI stands for the Glycemic Index. Foods containing carbohydrates have an effect on blood sugar levels and can be distinguished by either a high- or low-level GI.

Foods with a high GI value release sugar into the bloodstream quickly, giving you that familiar "sugar rush." This rise in blood sugar, however, doesn't last very long and quickly leaves you feeling tired, hungry, and low in energy.

Foods with a low GI value, however, release sugar into the bloodstream slowly, supplying a slow, steady source of energy. This leaves you feeling satisfied for a longer period of time, which in turn results in less snacking throughout the day.

The recipes in this book tend to include lots of GI foods, such as whole-wheat pasta, legumes, pulses, lentils, yogurt, fruits, and vegetables.

starchy foods

Starchy foods are an important part of a healthy diet. They include foods such as pasta, rice, cereals, and bread and are a vital part of any meal, as they provide a great source of energy and essential nutrients. Try to choose whole grain and whole-wheat varieties of starchy foods, such as whole-wheat pasta and couscous, brown rice, and whole-wheat bread, as they have a low GI value and will keep you feeling satisfied for longer.

fish

Eating plenty of fish will help ensure that your body is getting lots of important vitamins and minerals. We are recommended to eat a minimum of two portions of fish a week, of which at least one should be from an oily fish, which is high in omega-3 fats. Oily fish include tuna, salmon, mackerel, herring, and sardines. It's a good idea to try steaming or poaching your fish, in order to retain as many nutrients as possible.

fats

Not all fats are bad. Some are essential when eating a healthy, balanced diet. Our bodies

cannot provide us with all the essential fatty acids that we need to stay healthy, so it is important to include them in our diets. Extra virgin olive and canola oils are a great source of unsaturated fats, which are also found naturally in oily fish, nuts, and seeds. It is recommended to avoid eating too many saturated fats, as there are fears that they could increase the risk of high cholesterol and coronary heart disease.

salt and sugar

Salt and sugar are two foods that it is advisable to cut back on. To reduce the risk of getting high blood pressure, and therefore reduce the risk of strokes and heart disease, it is important not to eat too much salt. Try flavoring food with herbs, spices, and lemon juice, and always taste your food before automatically adding salt.

Added sugar is an ingredient that our bodies can do without. Try instead to get sweetness from foods that have naturally occurring sugars in them, such as fruit, and if you do need to add sugar, try to use the least refined sorts possible. Palm sugar and agave nectar are less processed alternatives.

fiber

Fiber is a vital part of a healthy diet if you want to avoid constipation, bowel cancer, and various other digestive problems. As well as the more obvious foods, such as breads, pasta, rice, and potatoes, fruit and vegetables

also have lots of natural dietary fiber. To boost your intake, try adding a portion of raw vegetable salad or a handful of crushed whole nuts to your meal.

protein and dairy

Protein is essential for the repair and growth of our bodies. As well as lean meat and fish, try to include eggs and legumes in your diet—all are great sources of protein. Dairy produce is also a good source of protein as well as calcium, essential for keeping our bones healthy. Try drinking skim milk, which contains the same amount of calcium as whole milk, but less saturated fats.

11

some healthy cooking methods

- Steaming is a gentle way to cook vegetables, fish, and lean cuts of meat, ensuring a great texture while locking the nutrients in. Whether you want to cook with a fancy electric steamer, a simple steamer basket, or an Asian-style bamboo steamer, this is one of the healthiest forms of cooking.

- Poaching in liquid is also a great way of cooking fish and meat while keeping it tender and moist. It's really versatile way of cooking, and the combinations of flavors you can use when poaching are endless.

- Broiling or grilling is a healthy form of cooking fattier cuts of meat, as it allows the fat to melt away from the meat and run off, leaving you with a delicious grilled taste, but without the excess fat. Using a heavy, ridged griddle pan is also a great way to cook vegetables, such as strips of eggplant and zucchini, without having to add extra oil while cooking.

- Stir-frying is a really healthy way of cooking food quickly while retaining texture, taste, and nutrients. You only need to use small amounts of oil in a well-seasoned wok or large skillet over a very high heat. Stir-frying is the ultimate healthy way of cooking "fast food."

- Slow cooking, either in a slow cooker designed especially for the purpose, or in a casserole in the oven or on the stovetop, is a perfect way of cooking some of the tougher cuts of meat, without compromising on taste. The long, slow, gentle cooking allows the flavors to really develop while giving the meat really drop-off-the-bone tenderness. You can then skim any excess fat from the top of the dish when it has finished cooking.

tips for healthy eating

- Do invest in a really good, nonstick skillet. It will drastically reduce the amount of oil you will need to cook with.

- Don't skip breakfast! Eating breakfast in the morning is a chance to refuel your body and get your metabolism going. This is essential if you want to keep your energy levels high while avoiding the trap of snacking throughout the morning.

- Do try using an olive oil spray to grease your pans and bakeware. It is an easier way to control how much oil you use, both for cooking and on salads.

- Don't do diets that are going to make your weight "yo-yo." Rapid weight loss can be more damaging to your health, and weight is much more likely to go back on once the diet is finished. It is much healthier for both body and mind to make some simple changes to the way that you cook and eat. If you eat healthily and exercise sensibly, you will be much more likely to reach your goal weight and stick to it.

- Do replace high sugar or salty snacks with more natural alternatives. Eaten in moderation, nuts, seeds, and dried fruits are much healthier snacks and likely to satisfy any cravings. Try cutting up raw vegetables into batons and serving with fat-free thick yogurt mixed with fresh herbs and lemon juice for a totally guilt-free evening snack.

- Don't overseason your food with salt or sugar during cooking; if you do, it cannot be removed. Instead, season lightly during the cooking process and encourage your family to add a squeeze of lemon juice or some extra spices to replace any extra salt, which is bad for your health in large quantities.

- Do exercise! We are recommended to do at least 30 minutes of exercise each day in order to stay fit and healthy. Low-impact activities, such as walking, yoga, aerobics, and swimming, are all great ways to introduce a little exercise into your life without risking damage to joints.

breakfast & brunch

oatmeal with prune compote

Serves 4–8
Preparation time **5 minutes**
Cooking time **about
   20 minutes**

4 cups **skim** or **low-fat milk**
2 cups **water**
1 teaspoon **vanilla extract**
pinch of **ground cinnamon**
pinch of **salt**
2 cups **rolled oats**
3 tablespoons **slivered
   almonds**, toasted

Compote
1 1/3 cups **ready-to-eat dried
   Agen prunes**
1/2 cup **apple juice**
1 small **cinnamon stick**
1 **clove**
1 tablespoon **mild agave
   nectar** or **honey**
1 unpeeled **orange** quarter

Place all the compote ingredients in a small saucepan over a medium heat. Simmer gently for 10–12 minutes or until softened and slightly sticky. Allow to cool. (The compote can be prepared in advance and chilled.)

Put the milk, measurement water, vanilla extract, cinnamon, and salt in a large saucepan over a medium heat and bring slowly to a boil. Stir in the oats, then reduce the heat and simmer gently, stirring occasionally, for 8–10 minutes until creamy and tender.

Spoon the porridge into bowls, sprinkle with the almonds, and serve with the prune compote.

For sweet quinoa oatmeal with banana & dates,
put 1 1/3 cups quinoa in a saucepan with the milk, agave nectar or honey, and 2–3 cardamom pods. Simmer gently for 12–15 minutes or until the quinoa is cooked and the desired consistency is reached. Serve in bowls topped with dollops of fat-free plain yogurt, 1/2 cup chopped dates, and freshly sliced banana.

bacon & mushroom frittata

Serves **4**

Preparation time **5 minutes**

Cooking time **25–30 minutes**

8 **portabella** or **flat chestnut mushrooms**, about 1 lb in total

1 **garlic clove**, finely chopped (optional)

olive oil spray

4 lean **Canadian bacon slices**

6 large **eggs**

1 tablespoon **chopped chives**, plus extra to garnish

1 tablespoon **whole grain mustard**

knob of **butter**

4 large slices of **sourdough bread**

salt and **pepper**

Put the mushrooms on a foil-lined baking sheet and sprinkle over the garlic, if using. Spray with a little olive oil, season with salt and pepper, and place in a preheated oven, 350°F, for 18–20 minutes or until softened. Leave until cool enough to handle.

Meanwhile, lay the bacon slices on a foil-lined broiler pan and cook under a preheated medium-hot broiler for 5–6 minutes, turning once or until slightly crispy. Cool slightly, then slice thickly.

Put the eggs, chives, and mustard in a bowl, beat together lightly and season with pepper.

Heat a large, nonstick skillet with an ovenproof handle, add the butter and melt until beginning to froth. Pour in the egg mixture and cook for 1–2 minutes, then add the bacon and whole mushrooms, stalk side up. Cook for an additional 2–3 minutes or until almost set. Place the pan under a preheated hot broiler and cook the frittata for 2–3 minutes until set, then cool slightly.

Toast the bread and arrange on serving plates. Cut the frittata into wedges and serve on the toasted sourdough, garnished with chives.

For mushroom & bacon quiche, roll out 12 oz prepared, whole-wheat short pastry to fit a lightly greased 9 inch tart pan and bake blind (i.e. bake the empty shell without filling) in the preheated oven for 12–15 minutes or until lightly golden. Cook the mushrooms and bacon as above and sprinkle over the pastry shell. Fill with the beaten egg mixture and return to the oven for 25–30 minutes or until risen and cooked.

granola with peaches & yogurt

Serves 4
Preparation time **15 minutes**,
    plus cooling
Cooking time **45 minutes**

2 cups **rolled oats**
½ cup **wheat germ**
⅓ cup **sunflower seeds**
¼ cup **sesame seeds** or
    flax seeds
½ cup **pumpkin seeds**
⅓ cup **whole blanched**
    almonds
⅓ cup **hazelnuts**
½ teaspoon **ground**
    cinnamon
½ teaspoon **ground apple**
    pie spice
¼ teaspoon **salt**
½ cup **maple syrup**
1 tablespoon **molasses**
2 tablespoons **vegetable** or
    canola oil
½ cup chopped **ready-to-eat**
    dried apricots, chopped
½ cup **dried cranberries**
⅓ cup **golden raisins**
1 ½ cups **fat-free plain yogurt**
2 **peaches**, pitted and sliced

Mix together the cereals, seeds, nuts, spices, and salt in a large bowl.

Heat the maple syrup, molasses, oil, and 2 tablespoons water in a small saucepan, then pour over the dry ingredients. Stir until thoroughly combined.

Tip the mixture onto a large, lightly oiled baking sheet, then press down firmly to make clumps. Place in a preheated oven, 275°F, for about 30 minutes. Add the dried fruits and stir gently to combine. Return to the oven for an additional 15 minutes or until evenly crisp and golden brown.

Allow to cool on the baking sheet (it will continue to crisp up as it cools), then store in an airtight container for up to 1 week. To serve, spoon into serving bowls and top with the yogurt and peaches.

For no-sugar toasted muesli, put the rolled oats, wheat germ, sunflower seeds, and chopped nuts in a large, nonstick skillet in batches and dry-fry. Stir in the cinnamon and apple pie spice and let cool completely before storing in an airtight container. To serve, spoon into bowls and add dried or fresh fruit, if desired.

herby smoked salmon omelets

Serves **4**
Preparation time **10 minutes**
Cooking time **about
   15 minutes**

8 **large eggs**
2 **scallions**, thinly sliced
2 tablespoons **chopped
   chives**
2 tablespoons **chopped
   chervil**
4 tablespoons **butter**
4 thin slices of **smoked
   salmon**, cut into thin strips,
   or 4 oz **smoked salmon
   trimmings**
pepper

Put the eggs, scallions, and herbs in a bowl, beat
together lightly, and season with pepper.

Heat a medium skillet over a medium-low heat, add a
quarter of the butter and melt until beginning to froth.
Pour in a quarter of the egg mixture and swirl to cover
the base of the pan. Stir gently for 2–3 minutes or until
almost set.

Sprinkle with a quarter of the smoked salmon strips
and cook for 30 seconds more or until just set. Fold
over and slide onto a serving plate. Repeat to make
3 more omelets. Serve each omelet immediately with
baby leaf and herb salad.

For smoked ham & tomato omelet, make as above,
adding 8–12 quartered cherry tomatoes to the egg
mixture. Replace the smoked salmon with 4 thin slices
of smoked ham, cut into strips.

fruity summer smoothie

Makes **4 x 1¼ cup glasses**
Preparation time **2 minutes**

2 **peaches**, halved, pitted, and
chopped
2 cups **strawberries**
2½ cups **raspberries**
1¾ cups **skim** or **lowfat milk**
ice cubes

Put the peaches in a blender or food processor with
the strawberries and raspberries and blend to a smooth
puree, scraping the mixture down from the sides of the
bowl if necessary.

Add the milk and blend the ingredients again until the
mixture is smooth and frothy. Pour the milkshake over
the ice cubes in tall glasses.

For soy milk & mango shake, replace the peaches,
strawberries, and raspberries with 2 large ripe mangoes
and the juice of 2 oranges. Puree as above, then pour
in 1⅓ cups soy milk, blend, and serve over ice cubes as
above.

home-baked seeded rolls

Makes **8 rolls**
Preparation time **25 minutes,**
 plus rising
Cooking time **12–15 minutes**

4 cups **all-purpose** or
 bread flour
½ cup **mixed seeds**
1 teaspoon **instant dry yeast**
1 teaspoon **sugar**
1 teaspoon **salt**
1 cup plus 2 tablespoons
 hand-hot water
1 tablespoon **melted butter**

Put the flour, seeds, and yeast in a large bowl, then stir in the sugar and salt. Pour in the measurement water and butter and mix to a dough. Turn the dough out on a lightly floured surface and knead for 5–10 minutes or until smooth and elastic.

Place in a lightly oiled bowl, cover with a clean, slightly damp dish towel and leave in a warm place to rise for at least 1 hour or until doubled in size. Alternatively, make the dough in a bread machine according to the manufacturer's instructions.

Push the dough back down and then divide into 8 balls. Knead each piece until smooth and round, then place evenly spaced on a large, lightly greased baking sheet. Cut a deep cross in each one, cover again with the damp dish towel, and leave in a warm place to rise for 1 hour or until doubled in size.

Bake the rolls in a preheated oven, 400°F, for 12–15 minutes or until golden and crusty and the rolls sound hollow when tapped on the underside. Cool slightly on a wire rack, pulling apart if they have spread during rising or cooking. Serve warm, split in half, with a bowl of thick-cut orange marmalade and a glass of freshly squeezed fruit juice, if desired.

For mixed seed loaf, make the dough as above but form into 1 large, round loaf. Allow to rise until doubled in size and then cook in the oven for 30 minutes or until golden and crusty and the loaf sounds hollow when tapped on the underside. Cool on a wire rack. Cut into slices and serve warm or toasted.

banana muffins

Makes **12**
Preparation time **10 minutes**
Cooking time **20–22 minutes**

1¾ cups **all-purpose flour**
½ cup **bran**
⅓ cup **soft dark brown sugar**
1 teaspoon **baking powder**
¾ teaspoon **baking soda**
½ teaspoon **ground apple pie spice** (optional)
¾ cup **buttermilk**
2½ tablespoons **peanut oil**
2 **large eggs**, beaten
1 teaspoon **vanilla extract**
2 small, **very ripe bananas**, peeled and mashed

Mix together the dry ingredients in a large bowl. Stir together the remaining ingredients in a separate bowl, then pour the wet ingredients onto the dry mixture and stir with a large metal spoon until just combined.

Spoon the mixture into a lightly greased large, 12-cup nonstick muffin pan for smaller muffins, or alternatively, a 6-cup pan for larger muffins, and bake in a preheated oven, 350°F, for 20–22 minutes or until risen and golden and a skewer inserted into the centers comes out clean.

Transfer to a wire rack to cool slightly. Serve the still-warm muffins with glasses of freshly squeezed fruit juice, if desired.

For banana, blueberry, & wheat germ muffins,
make as above, replacing 1 of the bananas with 1 cup blueberries, the bran with ⅓ cup wheat germ and the apple pie spice with ½ teaspoon ground cinnamon.

poached eggs & spinach

Serves **4**
Preparation time **5 minutes**
Cooking time **8–10 minutes**

4 strips of **cherry tomatoes**
   on the vine, about
   6 tomatoes on each
2 tablespoons **balsamic syrup**
   or **glaze**
1 small bunch of **basil**, leaves
   removed
1 tablespoon **distilled vinegar**
4 large **eggs**
4 thick slices of **whole-wheat
   bread**
reduced-fat butter, to spread
   (optional)
2 cups **baby leaf spinach**
salt and **pepper**

Lay the cherry tomato vines in an ovenproof dish, drizzle with the balsamic syrup or glaze, sprinkle with the basil leaves, and season with salt and pepper. Place in a preheated oven, 350°F, for 8–10 minutes or until the tomatoes begin to collapse.

Meanwhile, bring a large saucepan of water to a gentle simmer, add the vinegar, and stir with a large spoon to create a swirl. Carefully break 2 eggs into the water and cook for 3 minutes. Remove with a slotted spoon and keep warm. Repeat with the remaining eggs.

Toast the whole-wheat bread and butter lightly, if desired.

Heap the spinach onto serving plates and top each plate with a poached egg. Arrange the vine tomatoes on the plates, drizzled with any cooking juices. Serve immediately with the whole-wheat toast, cut into fingers.

For spinach, egg, & cress salad, gently lower the unshelled eggs into a saucepan of simmering water. Cook for 7–8 minutes, then cool quickly under running cold water. Shell the eggs and slice thickly. Arrange the egg slices over the spinach leaves and halved cherry tomatoes. Sprinkle with ½ cup salad cress and serve with a little olive oil and balsamic syrup.

appetizers &
light bites

carrot & cashew nut salad

Serves **4**
Preparation time **10 minutes**
Cooking time **6–10 minutes**

½ cup **unsalted cashew nuts**
2 tablespoons **black mustard seeds**
1 lb **carrots**, peeled and coarsely grated
1 **red bell pepper**, cored, seeded, and thinly sliced
3 tablespoons chopped **chervil**
2 **scallions**, finely sliced

Dressing
2 tablespoons **avocado oil**
2 tablespoons **raspberry vinegar**
1 tablespoon **whole grain mustard**
pinch of **sugar**
salt and **pepper**

Heat a nonstick skillet over a medium-low heat and dry-fry the cashew nuts for 5–8 minutes, stirring frequently, or until golden brown and toasted. Tip onto a small plate and allow to cool. Add the mustard seeds to the pan and dry-fry for 1–2 minutes or until they start to pop.

Mix together the mustard seeds, carrots, bell pepper, chervil, and scallions in a large bowl.

Beat together all the dressing ingredients in a small bowl, then pour onto the grated carrot salad. Mix thoroughly to coat and heap into serving bowls.

Chop the cashew nuts coarsely and sprinkle over the salad. Serve immediately.

For carrot & celeriac coleslaw, mix together 1⅔ cups grated carrot and 1¼ cups coarsely grated celeriac with the mustard seeds, chervil, scallions, and dressing, omitting the bell pepper. Replace the cashew nuts with ½ cup chopped walnuts and serve as above.

fig, bean, & toasted pecan salad

Serves **4**

Preparation time **5 minutes**,
plus cooling

Cooking time **5–6 minutes**

1 cup **pecan nuts**

2 cups **green beans**, trimmed

4 **fresh figs**, cut into quarters

2½ cups **arugula leaves**

small handful of **mint leaves**

2 oz **Parmesan** or **pecorino
cheese**

Dressing

3 tablespoons **walnut oil**

2 teaspoons **sherry vinegar**

1 teaspoon **vincotto**

salt and **pepper**

Heat a heavy skillet over a medium heat, add the pecan nuts and dry-fry, stirring frequently, for 3–4 minutes or until browned. Tip onto a small plate and allow to cool.

Cook the beans in a saucepan of lightly salted boiling water for 2 minutes. Drain, refresh under running cold water, and pat dry with paper towels. Put the beans in a bowl with the figs, pecan nuts, argula, and mint.

Beat together all the dressing ingredients in a small bowl and season with salt and pepper. If you can't find vincotto, use balsamic vinegar as an alternative. Pour over the salad and toss well. Shave over the Parmesan or pecorino and serve.

For mixed bean salad, combine 2 cups cooked trimmed green beans with 2 x 13 oz cans drained mixed beans, 4 finely chopped scallions, 1 crushed garlic clove, and 4 tablespoons chopped mixed herbs, then dress with 4 tablespoons olive oil, juice of ½ lemon, a pinch of superfine sugar, and salt and pepper.

watermelon, feta, & herb salad

Serves **4**
Preparation time **15 minutes**

¼ **watermelon**, about
1¾ lb 10 oz in total, peeled
and cut into large chunks
1 small bunch of **parsley**, finely
chopped
1 small bunch of **mint**, finely
chopped
1 small bunch of **cilantro**,
finely chopped
7 oz **reduced-fat feta cheese**,
cubed
16 pitted **Greek olives**
1 tablespoon **red jalapeño
peppers in brine**, drained
and finely chopped
juice of 1 **lime**, plus extra
wedges, to serve
small handful of **alfalfa** or
radish shoots, to garnish

Put the watermelon, herbs, feta, olives, and jalapeño peppers in a large bowl and toss together.

Spoon into serving dishes and pour over the lime juice. Garnish with the alfalfa or radish shoots and serve with lime wedges and grissini breadsticks, if desired.

For watermelon fruit salad, mix together the watermelon and chopped mint with 2 peeled, sliced kiwifruit, 1¼ cups red grapes, halved, 2 small, peeled, cored, and thinly sliced apples, and 1 cup pitted cherries, if in season. Dust with a little confectioners' sugar, if desired, and squeeze over the lime juice. Serve chilled.

roasted summer vegetables

Serves **4**

Preparation time **15 minutes**

Cooking time **45–50 minutes**

1 **red bell pepper**, cored,
    seeded, and thickly sliced

1 **yellow bell pepper**, cored,
    seeded, and thickly sliced

1 **eggplant**, cut into chunks

2 **yellow** or **green zucchini**,
    cut into chunks

1 **red onion**, cut into wedges

6 **garlic cloves**

5 oz **yellow** and **red baby
    plum tomatoes**

2 tablespoons **extra virgin
    canola** or **olive oil**

4–5 **thyme sprigs**

1 cup **hazelnuts**

2½ cups **arugula leaves**

2 tablespoons **raspberry** or
    balsamic vinegar

salt and **pepper**

handful of **mustard cress**,
    to garnish (optional)

Toss all the vegetables, except the tomatoes, in a large bowl with the oil. Season with a little salt and pepper and add the thyme. Tip into a large roasting pan and place in a preheated oven, 375°F, for 40–45 minutes or until the vegetables are tender. Add the tomatoes and return to the oven for an additional 5 minutes or until the tomatoes are just softened and beginning to burst.

Meanwhile, tip the hazelnuts into a small roasting pan and place in the oven for about 10–12 minutes or until golden and the skin is peeling away. Allow to cool, then remove the excess skin and crush lightly.

Toss the arugula leaves gently with the mixed, roasted vegetables and heap onto large plates. Sprinkle with the crushed hazelnuts and drizzle with the vinegar. Sprinkle over the mustard cress, if using, and serve immediately,

For roasted vegetable pasta sauce, roast the vegetables as above, then tip into a large saucepan with the tomatoes, 2 cups pureed tomatoes and ²/₃ cup vegetable stock. Bring to a boil, then reduce the heat and simmer gently for 20 minutes. Remove from the heat and use an immersion blender to blend until smooth. Season with salt and pepper, to taste, and serve with bowls of hot pasta. Alternatively, stir in an extra 1 cup vegetable stock to make soup.

middle eastern bread salad

Serves **4–6**
Preparation time **10 minutes**,
  plus cooling
Cooking time **2–3 minutes**

2 **whole-wheat flatbreads** or
  flour tortillas
1 large **green bell pepper**,
  cored, seeded, and diced
1 **Lebanese cucumber**, diced
15 **cherry tomatoes**, halved
½ **red onion**, finely chopped
2 tablespoons chopped **mint**
2 tablespoons chopped
  parsley
2 tablespoons chopped
  cilantro
3 tablespoons **olive oil**
juice of 1 **lemon**
salt and **pepper**

Toast the flatbreads or tortillas on a preheated ridged griddle pan or under a preheated hot broiler for 2–3 minutes or until charred. Allow to cool, then tear into bite-size pieces.

Put the bell pepper, cucumber, tomatoes, onion, and herbs in a serving bowl, add the oil and lemon juice, and season with salt and pepper, tossing well. Add the bread and stir again. Serve immediately.

For tomato & bread salad, chop 1½ lb tomatoes and put into a large bowl. Add 4 slices of diced day-old bread, 1 bunch of basil leaves, ⅔ cup pitted black olives, 5 tablespoons olive oil, 1 tablespoon balsamic vinegar, and salt and pepper. Toss well and serve.

pepper & eggplant hummus

Serves **4–6**
Preparation time **10 minutes,**
 plus cooling
Cooking time **45–50 minutes**

1 **red bell pepper,** cored,
 seeded, and quartered
3 **garlic cloves,** unpeeled and
 lightly crushed
1 **eggplant,** cut into large
 chunks
1 tablespoon **chili oil,** plus
 extra to serve
½ tablespoon **fennel seeds**
 (optional)
13 oz can **chickpeas,** drained
1 tablespoon **tahini**
1 teaspoon **sesame seeds,**
 lightly toasted
salt and **pepper**

To serve
4 **whole-wheat pita breads**
olive oil spray
1 teaspoon **paprika**

Put the pepper, garlic, and eggplant in a single layer in a large roasting pan. Drizzle with the chili oil and sprinkle with the fennel seeds, if using, and season with salt and pepper. Place in a preheated oven, 375°F, for 35–40 minutes or until softened and golden. Remove from the oven but do not turn it off.

Peel the skins from the garlic cloves and put in a food processor or blender with the roasted vegetables, three-quarters of the chickpeas, and the tahini. Blend until almost smooth, season to taste, and then spoon into a serving bowl. Cover with plastic wrap and allow to cool.

Cut the pita bread into 1 inch strips and place in a large bowl. Spray with a little olive oil and toss with the paprika and a little salt until well coated. Arrange in a single layer on a baking sheet. Toast in the oven for 10–12 minutes or until crisp.

Sprinkle the hummus with the remaining chickpeas and the sesame seeds and drizzle with 1–2 tablespoons chili oil. Serve with the toasted pita breads.

For roasted artichoke & pepper hummus, replace the eggplant with a drained 13 oz can artichoke hearts in water. Roast in the oven with the pepper and garlic, as above, replacing the chili oil with 1 tablespoon lemon-infused oil. Omit the fennel seeds. Continue as above.

chicken tikka sticks & fennel raita

Serves **6**
Preparation time **20 minutes**,
  plus marinating and chilling
Cooking time **8–10 minutes**

1 **onion**, finely chopped
½–1 large **red** or **green chili**,
  seeded and finely chopped
  (to taste)
¾ inch piece of **fresh ginger
  root**, finely chopped
2 **garlic cloves**, finely chopped
⅔ cup **fat-free plain yogurt**
3 teaspoons **mild curry paste**
4 tablespoons chopped
  cilantro
4 **chicken breasts**, about
  5 oz each, cubed

Fennel raita
1 small **fennel bulb**, about
  7 oz
¾ cup **fat-free plain yogurt**
3 tablespoons chopped
  cilantro
salt and **pepper**

Mix the onion, chili, ginger, and garlic together in a shallow china or glass dish. Add the yogurt, curry paste, and cilantro and mix together.

Add the cubed chicken to the yogurt mixture, mix to coat, cover with plastic wrap, and chill for at least 2 hours.

Make the raita. Cut the core away from the fennel and finely chop the remainder, including any green tops. Mix the fennel with the yogurt and cilantro and season with salt and pepper. Spoon the raita into a serving dish, cover with plastic wrap, and chill until needed.

Thread the chicken onto 12 skewers and place them on a foil-lined broiler rack. Cook under a preheated broiler for 8–10 minutes, turning once, or until browned and the chicken is cooked through. Transfer to serving plates and serve with the raita on the side.

For a red pepper & almond chutney, to serve with the skewers instead of the raita, blend ½ cup store-bought roasted peppers in a blender or food processor, with a handful of mint leaves, 1 chopped garlic clove, and ½ teaspoon chili powder. Blend until smooth, then add salt to taste and 1 ½ tablespoons toasted slivered almonds. Pulse a couple of times to roughly crush the almonds and stir in 1 tablespoon chopped cilantro.

salmon & cucumber sushi

Serves **4**

Preparation time **15 minutes**,
  plus cooling

Cooking time **about**
  15 minutes

1½ cups **sushi rice**

2 tablespoons **rice vinegar**

1 tablespoon **superfine sugar**

2 **nori sheets**

1 teaspoon **wasabi paste**

2 long strips of **cucumber**, the
  length of the nori and about
  ½ inch thick

4 oz **smoked salmon**

4 tablespoons **soy sauce**

2 tablespoons **pickled ginger**

Cook the sushi rice according to the package instructions.

Mix together the vinegar and sugar in a bowl and stir until the sugar dissolves. Once the rice is cooked, and when it is still warm, mix in enough of the vinegar and sugar mixture to coat the rice grains, but do not allow the rice to become wet. Tip the rice onto a tray to cool quickly.

Take 1 nori sheet and place it on a bamboo mat with the longest side in line with your body and the ridged surface facing upward. With damp hands, cover three-quarters of the nori sheet with a thin layer of rice, leaving a band of nori at the top without rice.

Spread a little wasabi paste with your finger on top of the rice in a thin line, at the edge nearest to you. Then place a cucumber strip and some smoked salmon on the wasabi.

Use the bamboo mat to start rolling the nori up, tucking in the cucumber and salmon as you go. Once you have rolled up the majority of the nori, wet your finger and dampen the plain edge of nori. Finish rolling up the nori. The wet edge will stick the roll together. Repeat with the other nori sheet. Then, using a sharp knife, cut the rolls into 8 even pieces or 4 even pieces and 1 slightly larger piece cut into 2 on the diagonal.

Mix the remaining wasabi and soy sauce and serve with the pickled ginger alongside the nori rolls.

turkey croque madame

Serves **4**
Preparation time **10 minutes**
Cooking time **8–10 minutes**

8 slices of **whole grain bread**
from a large, round loaf
3 tablespoons **whole grain mustard**
7 oz **aged Gruyère** or **reduced-fat sharp cheddar cheese**, finely grated
7 oz **cooked turkey**, thinly sliced
2 **tomatoes**, sliced
2 **scallions**, thinly sliced
4 tablespoons **low-fat cream cheese** (optional)
1 tablespoon **distilled vinegar**
4 **large eggs**
2 cups **baby leaf spinach**
pepper
chopped **chives**, to garnish

Lay 4 slices of the bread on a board and spread each slice with the mustard. Top the slices with half of the Gruyère or cheddar, the turkey and tomato slices, then sprinkle with the scallions. Season with pepper and sprinkle over the remaining Gruyère or cheddar. Spread the cream cheese, if using, over the remaining slices of bread and place, cheese side down, on top of the sandwiches.

Heat a large, nonstick skillet over a medium heat until hot, then carefully add the sandwiches and cook for 4–5 minutes or until golden and crispy. Turn the sandwiches over and cook for an additional 4–5 minutes. Alternatively, toast in a flat-surfaced panini machine according to the manufacturer's instructions.

Meanwhile, bring a large saucepan of water to a gentle simmer, add the vinegar and stir with a large spoon to create a swirl. Carefully break 2 eggs into the water and cook for 3 minutes. Remove with a slotted spoon and keep warm. Repeat with the remaining eggs.

Transfer each sandwich to a serving plate, sprinkle over a few spinach leaves and top with a poached egg. Garnish with chives and serve immediately.

For turkey & cheese sandwiches, cut 1 large whole grain baguette almost in half lengthwise. Cut into 4 and place, opened out, on a baking sheet. Top as above with the mustard, turkey, tomatoes, and scallions. Omit the cream cheese and finish with all of the grated cheese. Cook under a preheated hot broiler for 3–4 minutes or until hot and melted. Serve hot with baby leaf spinach and poached eggs, if desired.

lamb kefta pitas

Serves **4**
Preparation time **20 minutes**
Cooking time **10–12 minutes**

½ tablespoon **peanut oil**
4 **whole-wheat pita breads**
lemon juice, to serve

Lamb keftas
1 **small onion**, chopped
2 **garlic cloves**, crushed
13 oz **ground lamb**
1 cup **fresh whole-wheat
bread crumbs**
1 **small egg**, lightly beaten
1 small bunch of **parsley**,
chopped
1 small bunch of **cilantro**,
chopped
¼ tablespoon **ground
cinnamon**
1 tablespoon **ground paprika**
½ tablespoon **ground cumin**
salt and **pepper**

Salad
1 **carrot**, peeled and coarsely
grated
6 **radishes**, thinly sliced
½ **iceberg lettuce**, shredded
½ **cucumber**, thinly sliced

Place all the kefta ingredients in a food processor
and pulse several times until well combined. Tip into
a large bowl and, using wet hands, shape the mixture
into 16 meatballs.

Heat the oil in a large, nonstick skillet over a medium
heat, add the meatballs and then fry for 10–12 minutes,
turning frequently, until cooked through and browned
all over. Remove with a slotted spoon and drain on
paper towels.

Meanwhile, wrap the pita breads in foil and place in a
preheated oven, 350°F, for 5–8 minutes or until warm.
To make the salad, mix the carrot, radishes, lettuce, and
cucumber in a bowl.

Split open the warmed pitas, fill with the salad, and
then add the meatballs. Squeeze over a little lemon
juice and serve immediately.

For barbecued lamb skewers, make the kefta
mixture as above. Tip into a large bowl and form into
flat sausage shapes around 4 long, flat metal skewers.
Cook on a barbecue for 10–12 minutes or until cooked
through, then serve with the pita breads and salad
as above.

griddled chicken baguettes

Serves **4**
Preparation time **10 minutes**
Cooking time **8–10 minutes**

4 small **part-baked multigrain**
   or **seeded baguettes**
2 large boneless, skinless
   chicken breasts, about
   10 oz in total
1 teaspoon **olive oil**
4 tablespoons **red pepper**
   pesto
2 tablespoons **sunflower**
   seeds
handful of **arugula leaves**
salt and **pepper**

Salad
¼ **cucumber**, halved, seeded,
   and thinly sliced
2 tablespoons chopped **mint**
1 tablespoon **lemon juice**

Place the baguettes on a baking sheet and bake in a preheated oven, 400°F, for 8–10 minutes, or according to the package instructions, until crisp.

Meanwhile, lay a chicken breast between 2 sheets of plastic wrap and flatten with a rolling pin or meat mallet. Repeat with the remaining chicken breast. Heat a griddle pan over a medium-high heat until hot. Rub the oil over the chicken breasts, season with salt and pepper, and cook on the hot griddle for 2–3 minutes or until slightly charred. Turn the chicken breasts over and cook for an additional 2–3 minutes or until slightly charred and cooked through but not dry. Remove from the pan, cover with foil, and allow to rest.

Make the salad. Mix together the cucumber, mint, lemon juice, and a little salt and pepper in a small bowl.

Slice the chicken into thick slices. Cut the baguettes in half lengthwise, spread with the red pepper pesto, then fill with the chicken and the cucumber salad. Sprinkle with sunflower seeds and add a few arugula leaves. Cut in half and serve immediately.

For griddled chicken & spicy couscous, prepare and cook 4 chicken breasts as above and cut into thick slices. Meanwhile, cook 3 cups whole-wheat couscous according to the package instructions, then fork through 2 tablespoons harissa (see page 94 for homemade). Serve the chicken on the couscous with the cucumber salad as above.

felafel pita pockets

Serves **4**
Preparation time **15 minutes**,
   plus overnight soaking
Cooking time **12 minutes**

1½ cups **dried chickpeas**
1 **small onion**, finely chopped
2 **garlic cloves**, crushed
½ bunch of **parsley**
½ bunch of **cilantro**
2 teaspoons **ground
   coriander**
½ teaspoon **baking powder**
vegetable oil, for pan-frying
4 **whole-wheat pita breads**
handful of **salad leaves**
2 **tomatoes**, diced
4 tablespoons **fat-free plain
   yogurt**
salt and **pepper**

Put the chickpeas in a bowl, add cold water to cover by a generous 4 inches and allow to soak overnight.

Drain the chickpeas, transfer to a food processor and process until coarsely ground. Add the onion, garlic, fresh herbs, ground coriander, and baking powder. Season with salt and pepper and process until really smooth. Using wet hands, shape the mixture into 16 small patties.

Heat a little vegetable oil in a large skillet over a medium-high heat, add the patties, in batches, and fry for 3 minutes on each side or until golden and cooked through. Remove with a slotted spoon and drain on paper towels.

Split the pita breads and fill with the felafel, salad leaves, and diced tomatoes. Add a spoonful of the yogurt to each and serve immediately.

For felafel salad, toss 4 handfuls of mixed salad leaves with a little olive oil, lemon juice, and salt and pepper and arrange on serving plates. Core, seed, and dice 1 red bell pepper and sprinkle it over the salads. Top with the felafel and spoon over a little yogurt.

smoked mackerel crostini

Serves **4**
Preparation time **10 minutes**
Cooking time **2–3 minutes**

8 oz **smoked mackerel fillets**,
  skinned
1 tablespoon **creamed
  horseradish**
2 tablespoons **low-fat sour
  cream**
1 tablespoon chopped **chives**
finely grated zest of **1 lemon**
1 tablespoon **lemon juice**
1 **multigrain** or **seeded
  baguette**, sliced
1 **scallion**, finely sliced
  diagonally (optional)
4 crisp **baby lettuces**, leaves
  separated
pepper

Put the smoked mackerel in a bowl and break into flakes with a fork. Add the horseradish, sour cream, chives, lemon zest and juice, and plenty of pepper and mix together gently.

Place the sliced baguette on a broiler pan and cook under a preheated medium-hot broiler for 2–3 minutes or until crisp and golden, turning once. Serve the hot crostini immediately with the smoked mackerel rillettes, scallion, if desired, and the lettuce leaves.

For smoked mackerel fishcakes, mix the flaked mackerel with 1 cup cold mashed potato, 1 1/2 tablespoons horseradish, the chives, lemon zest and pepper, omitting the sour cream and lemon juice. Chill for 1 hour. Form into 4 patties with slightly damp hands, then dust in flour. Blitz the baguette in a food processor or blender to make bread crumbs. Dip each fishcake in beaten egg and coat in the bread crumbs. Heat a little extra virgin canola oil in a skillet, add the fishcakes, and fry for 4–5 minutes on each side or until cooked through and crisp. Drain on paper towels and serve with mixed salad leaves.

tuna & jalapeño baked potatoes

Serves **4**

Preparation time **10 minutes**, plus cooling

Cooking time **1 hour 5 minutes**

4 large **baking potatoes**

2 x 5½ oz cans **tuna** in spring water, drained

2 tablespoons drained and chopped **green jalapeño peppers** in brine

2 **scallions**, finely chopped

4 firm, ripe **tomatoes**, seeded and chopped

2 tablespoons chopped **chives**

3 tablespoons **low-fat sour cream**

1 cup grated **reduced-fat sharp cheddar cheese**

salt and **pepper**

Prick the potatoes all over with the tip of a sharp knife and place directly in a preheated oven, 350°F, for 1 hour or until crisp on the outside and the inside is tender. Leave until cool enough to handle.

Cut the potatoes in half and scoop the cooked flesh into a bowl. Place the empty potato skins, cut side up, on a baking sheet. Mix the tuna, jalapeño peppers, scallions, tomatoes, and chives into the potato in the bowl. Gently fold in the sour cream, then season with salt and pepper to taste.

Spoon the filling into the potato skins, sprinkle with the cheddar and cook under a preheated medium-hot broiler for 4–5 minutes or until hot and melted. Serve immediately with a frisée salad.

For spicy tuna wraps, spoon 4 tablespoons chunky spicy tomato salsa onto 4 large, whole-wheat flour tortillas. Sprinkle with the tuna, jalapeño peppers, and scallions. Omit the tomatoes, chives, and cheddar and top with ½ shredded iceberg lettuce. Roll up the wraps tightly and cut in half diagonally. Serve with a little low-fat sour cream, if desired.

soups & stews

spring minestrone

Serves **4–6**
Preparation time **15 minutes**
Cooking time **55 minutes**

2 tablespoons **olive oil**
1 **onion**, thinly sliced
2 **carrots**, peeled and diced
2 **celery sticks**, diced
2 **garlic cloves**, peeled
1 **potato**, peeled and diced
¾ cup **peas** or **fava beans**,
   thawed if frozen
1 **zucchini**, diced
1¼ cups **green beans**,
   trimmed and cut into
   1½ inch pieces
4 oz **plum tomatoes**, skinned
   and chopped
5 cups **vegetable stock**
¾ cup **small pasta shapes**
10 **basil leaves**, torn
salt and **pepper**

To serve
olive oil
grated **Parmesan cheese**

Heat the oil in a large, heavy saucepan over a low heat, add the onion, carrots, celery, and garlic and cook, stirring occasionally, for 10 minutes. Add the potato, peas or fava beans, zucchini, and green beans and cook, stirring frequently, for 2 minutes. Add the tomatoes, season with salt and pepper, and cook for an additional 2 minutes.

Pour in the stock and bring to a boil, then reduce the heat and simmer gently for 20 minutes or until all the vegetables are very tender.

Add the pasta and basil to the soup and cook, stirring frequently, until the pasta is al dente. Season with salt and pepper to taste.

Ladle into bowls, drizzle with olive oil, and sprinkle with the Parmesan. Serve with toasted country bread or Parmesan toasts (see below).

For Parmesan toasts, to serve as an accompaniment, toast 4–6 slices of ciabatta on one side only under a preheated medium broiler. Brush the other side with 2–3 tablespoons olive oil and sprinkle with dried red pepper flakes and 2 tablespoons grated Parmesan cheese, then cook under the preheated broiler until golden and crisp.

chicken & tofu miso noodles

Serves **4**
Preparation time **10 minutes**
Cooking time **25 minutes**

½ oz packets **instant miso
   soup powder** or **paste**
3 cups **water**
2 **star anise**
2 tablespoons **fish sauce**
1 tablespoon **light soy sauce**
1 tablespoon **palm sugar** or
   light brown sugar
1 **red chili**, seeded and sliced
   (optional)
7 oz **baby corn**
1 cup **snow peas**
8 oz **cooked chicken breast**,
   torn
7 oz **firm silken tofu**, cut into
   ½ inch cubes
6 oz **enoki mushrooms**, or
   shiitake mushrooms, thinly
   sliced
13 oz **fresh egg noodles**
1 **scallion**, very finely sliced,
   to garnish (optional)

Place the miso powder or paste in a large saucepan
with the measurement water, star anise, fish sauce,
soy sauce, sugar, and chili, if using. Bring to a boil, then
reduce the heat and simmer gently for 15 minutes.

Stir in the baby corn and snow peas and cook for an
additional 3 minutes or until almost tender. Remove
the pan from the heat, stir in the chicken, tofu, and
mushrooms and cover to retain the heat.

Cook the noodles in a large saucepan of boiling
water for 3–4 minutes, or according to the package
instructions, until tender. Drain well and divide between
deep bowls, then ladle over the hot soup and serve
immediately, garnished with the scallion, if desired.

For chicken, tofu, & mushroom stir-fry, heat
2 tablespoons peanut oil in a smoking hot wok or
large skillet. Stir-fry the baby corn and snow peas for
2 minutes or until beginning to wilt. Add the chicken,
tofu, and mushrooms and stir-fry for 1–2 minutes or
until hot and the mushrooms are tender. Stir in an
11½ oz jar of black bean stir-fry sauce, toss briefly and
serve with the cooked noodles, sprinkled with scallions.

squash, kale, & mixed bean soup

Serves **6**
Preparation time **15 minutes**
Cooking time **45 minutes**

1 tablespoon **olive oil**
1 **onion**, finely chopped
2 **garlic cloves**, finely
    chopped
1 teaspoon **smoked paprika**
1 lb **butternut squash**, halved,
    seeded, peeled, and diced
2 small **carrots**, peeled and
    diced
1 lb **tomatoes**, skinned
    (optional) and roughly
    chopped
13 oz can **mixed beans**,
    drained
3¾ cups **vegetable** or
    chicken stock
²/₃ cup **low-fat sour cream**
1 cup **kale**, torn into bite-size
    pieces
salt and **pepper**

Heat the oil in a saucepan over a medium-low heat, add the onion and fry gently for 5 minutes. Stir in the garlic and smoked paprika and cook briefly, then add the squash, carrots, tomatoes, and mixed beans.

Pour in the stock, season with salt and pepper and bring to a boil, stirring frequently. Reduce the heat, cover, and simmer for 25 minutes or until the vegetables are tender.

Stir in the sour cream, then add the kale, pressing it just beneath the surface of the stock. Cover and cook for 5 minutes or until the kale has just wilted. Ladle into bowls and serve with warm garlic bread.

For cheesy squash, pepper, & mixed bean soup,
make as above, replacing the carrots with 1 cored, seeded, and diced red bell pepper. Pour in the stock, then add 2½ oz Parmesan cheese rinds and season. Cover and simmer for 25 minutes. Stir in the sour cream but omit the kale. Discard the Parmesan rinds, ladle the soup into bowls, and top with grated Parmesan.

pesto & lemon soup

Serves **6**
Preparation time **10 minutes**
Cooking time **25 minutes**

1 tablespoon **olive oil**
1 **onion**, finely chopped
2 **garlic cloves**, finely chopped
2 **tomatoes**, skinned and
  chopped
5 cups **vegetable stock**
3 teaspoons **pesto**, plus extra
  to serve
grated zest and juice of
  1 lemon
4 oz **broccoli**, cut into small
  florets, stems sliced
1 **zucchini**, diced
²/₃ cup **frozen green
  soybeans**
½ cup **small pasta shapes**
1 cup **spinach**, shredded
salt and **pepper**
handful of **basil leaves**,
  to garnish (optional)

Heat the oil in a saucepan over a medium-low heat, add the onion and fry gently for 5 minutes, stirring occasionally, until softened. Add the garlic, tomatoes, stock, pesto, lemon zest, and a little salt and pepper and bring to a boil, then reduce the heat and simmer gently for 10 minutes.

Add the broccoli, zucchini, soybeans, and pasta shapes and simmer for 6 minutes. Add the spinach and lemon juice and cook for an additional 2 minutes or until the spinach has just wilted and the pasta is al dente.

Ladle into bowls, top with extra spoonfuls of pesto, and sprinkle with basil leaves. Serve with warm olive or sun-dried tomato focaccia or ciabatta bread or Parmesan thins (see below).

For homemade Parmesan thins, to serve as an accompaniment, line a baking sheet with nonstick parchment paper, then sprinkle 1 cup grated Parmesan cheese into 18 well-spaced mounds. Cook in a preheated oven, 375°F, for about 5 minutes or until the cheese has melted and is just beginning to brown. Allow to cool and harden, then peel off the paper and serve on the side with the soup.

thai-style chicken soup

Serves **4**
Preparation time **10 minutes**
Cooking time **25 minutes**

4 cups **chicken stock**
4 tablespoons **Thai fish sauce**
1 tablespoon **palm sugar** or
  light brown sugar
2 **lemon grass stalks**, sliced
  in half lengthwise
2 oz **galangal** or **fresh ginger
  root**, peeled and finely sliced
1 large bunch of **cilantro**, finely
  chopped, leaves and stalks
  separate
8 oz boneless, skinless
  chicken thighs,
  cut into strips
7½ oz can **bamboo shoots**,
  drained (optional)
7 oz **vermicelli rice noodles**

Put the stock, fish sauce, sugar, lemon grass, and galangal or ginger in a large saucepan and bring to a boil, then reduce the heat and simmer gently for 15 minutes. Strain through a strainer to remove the galangal or ginger and lemon grass. Return the liquid to the pan and stir in the chopped cilantro stalks.

Add the chicken and simmer gently for an additional 4–5 minutes or until cooked through. Add the bamboo shoots, if using.

Meanwhile, put the noodles in a large saucepan of boiling water, turn off the heat and allow to stand for 4 minutes, or according to the package instructions, until tender. Drain well and divide between deep bowls. Ladle over the chicken soup, sprinkle with the chopped cilantro leaves and serve immediately.

For chicken & bamboo shoot curry, heat 1 tablespoon peanut oil in a wok or large skillet, add 2 tablespoons green curry paste and fry for 2 minutes, stirring constantly. Add 1¼ cups reduced-fat coconut milk and ⅔ cup chicken stock, the fish sauce, palm sugar, chopped cilantro stalks, and chicken, omitting the lemon grass and galangal or fresh ginger root. Simmer gently for about 10 minutes, or until the chicken is cooked through, adding the bamboo shoots 4 minutes before the end of the cooking time. Serve with the chopped cilantro leaves and steamed Thai rice.

lima bean & tomato soup

Serves **4**
Preparation time **10 minutes**
Cooking time **20 minutes**

3 tablespoons **olive oil**
1 **onion**, finely chopped
2 **celery sticks**, thinly sliced
2 **garlic cloves**, thinly sliced
2 x 13 oz cans **lima beans**,
  drained
4 tablespoons **sundried**
  tomato paste
3¾ cups **vegetable stock**
1 tablespoon chopped **thyme**
  or **rosemary**, plus extra
  leaves to garnish
salt and **pepper**
Parmesan cheese shavings,
  to serve

Heat the oil in a saucepan over a medium heat, add the onion and fry for 3 minutes or until softened. Add the celery and garlic and fry for 2 minutes.

Add the lima beans, sundried tomato paste, stock, rosemary or thyme, and season with salt and pepper. Bring to a boil, then reduce the heat, cover, and simmer gently for 15 minutes.

Ladle into bowls and serve sprinkled with the Parmesan and extra thyme or rosemary leaves. This soup makes a light main course served with bread and plenty of Parmesan.

For spiced carrot & lentil soup, heat 2 tablespoons oil in a saucepan, add 1 chopped onion, 2 crushed garlic cloves, and 2 cups chopped carrots and fry for 10 minutes. Add a 13 oz can lentils, drained, 2 teaspoons ground coriander, 1 teaspoon ground cumin, and 1 tablespoon chopped thyme and fry for 1 minute. Stir in 4 cups vegetable stock, a 13 oz can chopped tomatoes, and 2 teaspoons lemon juice and bring to a boil. Cover and simmer gently for 20 minutes. Put in a food processor or blender and blend until smooth, then return to the pan and warm through.

shrimp & pork wonton soup

Serves **4**
Preparation time **25 minutes**
Cooking time **5–6 minutes**

4 oz **ground pork**
5 oz **raw peeled shrimp**
4 **scallions**, finely chopped
1 **garlic clove**
½ inch piece of **fresh ginger root**, peeled and chopped
1 tablespoon **oyster sauce**
20 **wonton skins**
3 cups **chicken stock**
1 head of **Chinese greens**, shredded
1–2 tablespoons **fish sauce**

To serve
handful of **cilantro leaves**
1 tablespoon **sesame seeds**
lime wedges

Place the pork, shrimps, 2 of the scallions, the garlic, ginger, and oyster sauce in a food processor or blender and blend to a paste.

Take 1 of the wonton skins and place 1 teaspoon of the shrimp and pork mixture in the center. Dampen the edges of the skin with a little water and bring them up around the filling, enclosing it completely in a little bundle. Repeat with the remainder of the skins and shrimp and pork mixture.

Bring the stock to a boil in a large saucepan, then reduce the heat, add the wontons and simmer for 4–5 minutes. Remove 1 of the wontons and check that it has become firm to the touch, which will indicate that it is cooked.

Add the greens to the pan and cook for 1 minute, then season with the fish sauce.

Ladle into deep bowls and serve with a few cilantro leaves, a sprinkling of sesame seeds, and a lime wedge on the side.

For sesame wontons with soy dipping sauce, make the wontons as above and steam them in a bamboo steamer for 5 minutes. Remove the wontons from the steamer and sprinkle over 2 tablespoons sesame seeds. Make a dipping sauce by mixing together 3 tablespoons light soy sauce, 2 teaspoons peeled and grated fresh ginger root, 1 finely sliced red chili, and 1 tablespoon fish sauce.

hot & sour beef broth

Serves **4**
Preparation time **12 minutes**
Cooking time **about**
   15 minutes

4 cups **clear beef stock**
3 tablespoons **fish sauce**
1 tablespoon **rice vinegar**
1 tablespoon **lime juice**
1 tablespoon **palm sugar** or
   light brown sugar
1 **garlic clove**, sliced
1 inch piece of **fresh ginger**
   root, peeled and cut into very
   thin matchsticks
1 small **red chili**, seeded and
   finely sliced
1 **shallot**, thinly sliced
3 **kaffir lime leaves**, thinly
   shredded
2 teaspoons **tamarind paste**
4 oz **baby corn**, halved
   lengthwise
12 oz **beef tenderloin**, thinly
   sliced
1 **scallion**, finely sliced,
   to garnish

Put the stock, fish sauce, vinegar, lime juice, and palm sugar in a large saucepan and bring to a boil. Add the garlic, ginger, chili, shallot, lime leaves, tamarind paste, and baby corn, then reduce the heat and simmer gently for 10 minutes.

Stir in the beef tenderloin, then immediately ladle into bowls. Sprinkle with the scallion and serve immediately.

For hot & sour mushroom broth, replace the beef stock and beef tenderloin with 2 cups dried shiitake mushrooms soaked in 4 cups boiling vegetable stock for 15–20 minutes. Drain, reserving the soaking liquid, and slice the mushrooms, then make the broth as above.

vegetable broth & sea bass

Serves **4**

Preparation time **5 minutes**

Cooking time **7–8 minutes**

3 cups **chicken** or **vegetable stock**

1 **fennel bulb**, cut into 8 wedges, herby tops reserved (optional)

12 fine **asparagus spears**

1 cup **frozen peas**, thawed

1 cup **fava beans**, podded

2 tablespoons **olive oil**

4 **sea bass fillets**, about 7 oz each, skin on and pin-boned

small handful of **mint leaves**, torn

small handful of **basil leaves**, torn

salt and **pepper**

Put the stock in a large saucepan and bring to a boil. Add the fennel, reduce the heat, and simmer for 3 minutes or until almost tender. Add the asparagus, peas, and fava beans and cook for a 1–2 minutes. Season with salt and pepper.

Meanwhile, heat the oil in a skillet over a medium heat. Season the sea bass with salt and pepper and place, skin side down, in the pan. Cook for 3–4 minutes or until the skin is crispy, then turn the fish over and cook for a minute more.

Ladle the vegetable broth into bowls and sprinkle with a few torn mint and basil leaves. Top the broth with the pan-fried sea bass and reserved herby fennel tops, if desired, and serve.

For Thai broth with shrimp, peel and devein 1 lb raw jumbo shrimps, reserving the shells and heads. Heat 3 cups fish or chicken stock in a saucepan. Add the shrimp shells and heads, 2 roughly chopped lemon grass stalks, a 2 inch piece of fresh ginger root, 1 dried red chili, and 2 kaffir lime leaves. Remove the pan from the heat and allow the stock to infuse for 30 minutes. Strain the stock and return it to a clean saucepan. Add the shrimp and poach for 3–4 minutes or until they have turned pink and are cooked through. Add 4 oz sugar snap peas 1 minute before the end of the cooking time.

vegetable broth with pearl barley

Serves **4**
Preparation time **15 minutes**
Cooking time **1½ hours**

½ cup **pearl barley**
2 tablespoons **extra virgin canola oil**
1 large **onion**, finely chopped
2 **leeks**, trimmed, cleaned, and finely chopped
1 **celery stick**, finely chopped
1½ lb mixed root vegetables such as **parsnips**, **turnips**, **rutabagas**, **carrots**, and **potatoes**, evenly diced
5 cups **beef** or **vegetable stock**
1 **bouquet garni**
salt and **pepper**

Bring a large saucepan of water to a boil and pour in the pearl barley. Cook at a gentle simmer for 1 hour. Drain well.

Meanwhile, heat the oil in a large, heavy saucepan over a medium-low heat, add the onion, leeks, and celery and fry gently for 8–10 minutes or until softened but not browned. Add the root vegetables and cook for an additional 5 minutes, stirring regularly.

Pour in the stock, add the bouquet garni, and bring to a boil. Stir in the pearl barley, then reduce the heat and simmer for 25–30 minutes or until the vegetables and pearl barley are tender. Remove the bouquet garni and season to taste with salt and pepper. Ladle into bowls and serve with herby bread, if desired.

For creamy vegetable soup, make the broth as above, then use an immersion blender to blend the soup until smooth, adding extra stock if necessary. Stir in 3 tablespoons low-fat sour cream, sprinkle with thyme leaves, and serve with toasted herby bread croutons.

rustic tuscan bean stew

Serves **4**
Preparation time **12 minutes**
Cooking time **45–50 minutes**

1 tablespoon **olive oil**
1 **red onion**, finely chopped
2 **celery sticks**, thinly sliced
1 large **carrot**, peeled and
　finely chopped
1 **red bell pepper**, cored,
　seeded, and diced
2 **garlic cloves**, chopped
1 tablespoon **tomato paste**
½ cup **red wine**
3 cups **vegetable stock**
13 oz can **mixed beans** or
　Tuscan bean mix, drained
2–3 **thyme sprigs**, chopped
1 **rosemary sprig**, chopped
2 **bay leaves**
1 cup mini **whole-wheat**
　pasta shapes or **orzo**
salt and **pepper**

To serve (optional)
olive oil
grated **Parmesan cheese**

Heat the oil in a large, heavy saucepan over a medium-low heat, then add the onion, celery, carrot, bell pepper, and garlic and cook gently for 12–15 minutes or until softened. Add the tomato paste and wine and cook for an additional 2–3 minutes.

Stir in the stock, beans, thyme, rosemary, and bay leaves and season with salt and pepper. Bring to a boil, then reduce the heat and simmer gently for 20 minutes.

Stir in the pasta shapes and continue to simmer for about 12 minutes or until the pasta is al dente.

Ladle into bowls and serve with a drizzle of olive oil and sprinkled with the Parmesan, if desired.

For hearty Tuscan bean salad, cook the vegetables in the olive oil for 18–20 minutes or until very tender. Toss with the beans and chopped herbs in a large serving bowl and allow to cool. Stir in 3 seeded and chopped tomatoes and 1–2 tablespoons red wine vinegar, then season with salt and pepper to taste. Toss lightly with a mixed leaf salad and garnish with Parmesan cheese shavings.

spanish fish stew

Serves **4**
Preparation time **12 minutes**
Cooking time **about
  25 minutes**

2 tablespoons **olive oil**
1 large **red onion**, sliced
4 **garlic cloves**, chopped
1 teaspoon **smoked paprika**
  or **hot smoked paprika**
pinch of **saffron threads**
12 oz **angler fish fillet**, cut
  into chunks
8 oz **red mullet fillets**, cut into
  large chunks
3 tablespoons **dry** or **medium-
  dry Madeira**
1 cup **fish** or **vegetable stock**
2 tablespoons **tomato paste**
13 oz can **chopped tomatoes**
2 bay leaves
1½ lb **live mussels**, scrubbed
  and debearded (discard any
  that don't shut when tapped)
  or 8 oz **cooked shelled
  mussels**
salt and **pepper**
3 tablespoons chopped
  parsley, to garnish

Heat the oil in a large, heavy saucepan over a medium-low heat, add the onion and garlic and cook gently for 8–10 minutes or until softened.

Stir in the paprika and saffron and cook for an additional minute. Stir in the fish, then pour over the Madeira. Add the stock, tomato paste, tomatoes, and bay leaves and season with salt and pepper. Bring to a boil, then reduce the heat and simmer gently for 5 minutes.

Stir in the live mussels, cover, and cook over a low heat for about 3 minutes or until they have opened. Discard any that remain closed. Alternatively, if using cooked shelled mussels, simmer the stew for 2–3 minutes more, or until the fish is cooked and tender, then stir in the cooked mussels. Cook for 30 seconds or until the mussels are heated through and piping hot.

Ladle into bowls and sprinkle with the parsley. Serve immediately with crusty bread.

For pan-fried red mullet with tomato sauce, cook the onion and garlic with the spices as above. Pour in the Madeira and add the tomatoes, finely grated zest of ½ lemon, a pinch of sugar, and season with salt and pepper. Simmer for 15–20 minutes. Heat 1–2 tablespoons olive oil in a nonstick skillet, add 1 lb red mullet fillets, skin side down, and fry for 2–3 minutes or until crisp. Cover, reduce the heat, and cook for another 2 minutes or until the fish is just cooked through. Serve with the tomato sauce.

tomato & chorizo stew with clams

Serves **4**
Preparation time **15 minutes**
Cooking time **about**
  25 minutes

10 oz **chorizo** sausage,
  cut into chunks
1 teaspoon **coriander seeds**,
  crushed
1 tablespoon **fennel seeds**,
  crushed
1 **onion**, finely chopped
1 **red chili**, seeded and finely
  chopped
2 **garlic cloves**, finely chopped
3 tablespoons **white wine**
13 oz can **chopped tomatoes**
¾ cup **fish stock**
1 lb **live clams**, cleaned
  (discard any that don't shut
  when tapped)
small handful of **basil leaves**,
  to garnish

Heat a large saucepan over a high heat, add the chorizo and fry until the natural oil has been released and the chorizo is beginning to brown. Remove with a slotted spoon, leaving behind the oil, and set aside.

Add the coriander and fennel seeds to the chorizo oil and fry for 1 minute, then add the onion and chili and fry until the onion has softened but not browned. Add the garlic and fry for another minute.

Pour in the white wine and allow to bubble until just 1 tablespoon of liquid is left. Add the tomatoes and stock and bring to a boil, then return the chorizo to the pan. Tip in the clams, then cover and cook until the clams have opened. Discard any that remain closed.

Ladle into bowls, sprinkle with a few basil leaves, and serve with crusty bread, if desired.

For spicy bean stew with pan-fried porgy, make the stew as above, omitting the clams and chorizo and adding 13 oz can haricot beans and 13 oz can kidney beans, drained. Pan-fry 2 porgy fillets and serve with the bean stew.

french summer vegetable stew

Serves **4**

Preparation time **12 minutes**

Cooking time **about
25 minutes**

2 tablespoons **olive oil**

1 **fennel bulb**

3 **shallots**, sliced

3 **garlic cloves**, sliced

2 tablespoons **Pernod**

½ cup **dry white wine**

1 tablespoon chopped **chives**

1 tablespoon chopped **chervil**

1 teaspoon chopped **tarragon**

2 **zucchini**, halved lengthwise
and sliced

1 cup **fine green beans**,
trimmed

2 cups **vegetable stock**

16 large, **pitted green olives**

15 small **cherry tomatoes**,
mixed colors if possible

1 small bunch of **basil**, leaves
torn

2 lean **Canadian bacon
slices**, very thinly sliced
(optional)

salt and **pepper**

Heat the oil in a large, heavy saucepan over a medium heat. Cut the fennel into quarters lengthwise, remove the tough middle and slice each quarter into 3 wedges. Add to the pan and fry for 4–5 minutes or until beginning to soften and brown. Add the shallots and garlic and fry gently for an additional 4–5 minutes or until softened and lightly golden.

Stir in the Pernod, white wine, and chopped herbs and bubble for 1–2 minutes or until almost evaporated. Add the zucchini and green beans and stir well.

Add enough stock to almost cover the vegetables and top with the olives. Bring to a boil, then reduce the heat, cover, and simmer gently for 8–10 minutes or until the vegetables are almost tender. Stir in the tomatoes and basil leaves and simmer for an additional 3 minutes. Season to taste with salt and pepper.

Place a small, nonstick skillet over a high heat and add the bacon, if using. Fry for 3 minutes or until crisp. Remove with a slotted spoon and drain on paper towels.

Ladle the stew into bowls and sprinkle with the crispy bacon, if using. Serve with warm, crusty bread, if desired.

For fennel & olive salad, slice 2 fennel bulbs thinly and arrange on a serving plate. Mix together 2 tablespoons red wine vinegar and 3 tablespoons olive oil in a bowl and season with salt and pepper. Drizzle over the fennel and top with the olives. Scatter with 2 tablespoons chopped parsley and the crispy bacon, if liked.

farmhouse sausage & kale stew

Serves **4**
Preparation time **10 minutes**
Cooking time **40 minutes**

1 tablespoon **olive oil**

5 oz lean **smoked bacon**,
chopped

3–4 lean **herby pork
sausages**, about 8 oz
in total, thickly sliced

1 **onion**, chopped

3 **garlic cloves**, chopped

1 **leek**, trimmed, cleaned,
and sliced

13 oz can **chopped tomatoes**

2 tablespoons **tomato paste**

1 teaspoon **dried oregano**

pinch of **sugar**

1¼ cups **pale ale** or **chicken
stock**

1 large **potato**, about 10 oz,
peeled and roughly diced

13 oz can **cranberry beans**,
drained

2 cups shredded **kale**

salt and **pepper**

2 tablespoons chopped
parsley, to garnish

Heat the oil in a large, heavy saucepan over a medium-
high heat, add the bacon and sausages and cook for
3–4 minutes or until browned. Add the onion, garlic, and
leek, reduce the heat slightly and cook for 5–6 minutes
until softened, stirring occasionally.

Stir in the tomatoes, tomato paste, dried oregano,
sugar, and ale or stock and bring to a boil. Stir in
the potatoes and beans and season with salt and
pepper. Reduce the heat, cover, and simmer gently for
20 minutes or until the potatoes are almost tender. Stir
in the kale, check the seasoning, and cook for another
8–10 minutes or until the kale and potatoes are tender.

Ladle into bowls and sprinkle with the parsley. Serve
immediately.

For chicken & chorizo stew, make as above, replacing
the bacon with 5 oz diced chorizo, the sausages with
8 oz sliced boneless, skinless chicken thighs, the
oregano with 1 teaspoon smoked paprika, and the ale
or stock with 1¼ cups red wine. Serve sprinkled with
the parsley and a generous squeeze of lemon juice.

tunisian chickpea & lentil stew

Serves **4**
Preparation time **15 minutes**,
  plus overnight soaking
Cooking time **about 2¼ hours**

1¼ cups **dried chickpeas**
2 tablespoons **olive oil**
3 **garlic cloves**, thinly sliced
1 **onion**, thinly sliced
1 **celery stick**, finely diced
2 **small carrots**, peeled and
  finely diced
pinch of **saffron threads**
½ teaspoon **ground turmeric**
½ teaspoon **paprika**
1 teaspoon **ground cumin**
½ teaspoon **ground ginger**
¼ teaspoon **ground
  cinnamon**
½ cup **green lentils**, rinsed
2 tablespoons **tomato paste**
3 cups **lamb** or **vegetable
  stock**
salt and **pepper**
3–4 tablespoons chopped
  parsley, to garnish
harissa (see right for
  homemade), to serve

Put the chickpeas in a bowl, add cold water to cover by 4 inches and allow to soak overnight.

Drain the chickpeas, rinse under running cold water and drain again. Place the chickpeas in a saucepan of cold water and bring to a boil. Boil rapidly for 10 minutes, then reduce the heat and simmer gently, partially covered, for about 1 hour or until tender, adding more water as necessary. Drain well.

Meanwhile, heat the oil in a large, heavy saucepan over a medium-low heat, add the garlic, onion, celery, and carrots and cook for 15 minutes, or until softened, stirring frequently. Add the spices and stir-fry for 1–2 minutes, then increase the heat and add the chickpeas, lentils, and tomato paste. Pour in the stock and bring to a boil, then reduce the heat and simmer gently for 40–45 minutes.

Spoon the cooked legumes and vegetables into serving bowls and carefully pour the liquid around the side. Sprinkle with parsley and serve with harissa, to taste.

For homemade harissa, soak 1 oz dried red chilies in boiling water for 4 hours. Put 1½ tablespoons cumin seeds, 2 teaspoons caraway seeds, and 1 tablespoon coriander seeds in a small skillet and dry-fry until fragrant. Grind to a powder in a mini chopper. Add the soaked chilies, 3 garlic cloves, ½ cup roasted peppers, 2 tablespoons tomato paste, 1 tablespoon aged sherry vinegar, 1 teaspoon hot smoked paprika, 1 teaspoon salt, and just enough olive oil to make a paste. Blend until smooth, then store in an airtight jar in the refrigerator for up to 2–3 weeks.

harira

Serves **8–10**

Preparation time **about 25 minutes**, plus overnight soaking

Cooking time **about 2¾ hours**

1½ cups **dried chickpeas**

2 **chicken breasts**, halved

5 cups **chicken stock**

5 cups **water**

2 x 13 oz cans **chopped tomatoes**

¼ teaspoon crumbled **saffron threads** (optional)

2 **onions**, chopped

½ cup **long-grain rice**

¼ cup **green lentils**, rinsed

2 tablespoons finely chopped **cilantro**

2 tablespoons finely chopped **parsley**

salt and **pepper**

coriander sprigs, to garnish

fat-free plain yogurt, to serve

Put the chickpeas in a bowl, add cold water to cover by a generous 4 inches and leave to soak overnight. Drain the chickpeas, rinse under running cold water, and drain again. Place the chickpeas in a saucepan of cold water and bring to a boil. Boil rapidly for 10 minutes, then reduce the heat and simmer, partially covered, for about 1¾ hours or until tender, adding more water as necessary. Drain well.

Meanwhile, place the chicken breasts, stock, and measurement water in another saucepan and bring to a boil, then reduce the heat, cover, and simmer for 10–15 minutes or until the chicken is just cooked. Remove the chicken with a slotted spoon, reserving the stock, place it on a board and shred it, discarding the skin. Set aside.

Stir the chickpeas, tomatoes, saffron, if using, onions, rice, and lentils into the reserved stock in the pan, cover, and simmer for 30–35 minutes or until the rice and lentils are tender.

Add the shredded chicken, cilantro and parsley just before serving. Heat the soup for an additional 5 minutes without letting it boil. Season to taste with salt and pepper, then ladle into bowls, drizzle over the yogurt, and garnish with the cilantro.

For budget harira, make as above, omitting the chicken breasts and replacing the saffron with ½ teaspoon ground turmeric and ½ teaspoon ground cinnamon.

fish &
seafood

cod & eggplant tapenade

Serves **4**
Preparation time **12 minutes**
Cooking time **35–40 minutes**

1 **eggplant**, cut into chunks
1 **garlic clove**, sliced
olive oil spray
4 thick, line-caught **cod fillets**, about 5 oz each
finely grated zest of ½ **lemon**
2 teaspoons finely chopped **lemon thyme**
2 teaspoons **olive oil**
1–2 tablespoons **black olive tapenade**
1–2 tablespoons **fat-free plain yogurt**
2 tablespoons **pine nuts**, lightly toasted (optional)
salt and **pepper**

Put the eggplant in a foil-lined roasting pan, sprinkle with the garlic, season with salt and pepper, and spray with a little olive oil. Cover tightly with foil and place in a preheated oven, 350°F, for 35–40 minutes or until the eggplant is tender.

Meanwhile, place a cod fillet in the center of a piece of foil or nonstick parchment paper. Sprinkle with a little lemon zest, lemon thyme, and season with salt and pepper. Drizzle over ½ teaspoon of the olive oil, then fold the foil or paper over several times to make a small package. Repeat with the remaining cod fillets. Place the packages on a baking sheet and bake in the oven 12 minutes before the end of the eggplant cooking time, until the fish is just cooked through. Allow to rest.

Remove the eggplant from the oven and place in a food processor or blender with the black olive tapenade and yogurt. Blend until almost smooth, season to taste, and scrape into a bowl.

Serve the cod on a bed of steamed green beans, sprinkled with the pine nuts, if using, and with the eggplant and yogurt puree on the side.

For baked lemon sole & capers, place 4 lemon sole fillets on a large, foil-lined baking sheet. Sprinkle with the lemon zest, lemon thyme, and 1 teaspoon rinsed and drained capers, chopped. Drizzle with the olive oil, then season with pepper. Cover tightly with foil and place in the preheated oven for 8–10 minutes or until the fish is just cooked and flakes easily. Serve as above.

roasted haddock loins

Serves **4**
Preparation time **10 minutes**
Cooking time **about 1 hour**

4 thick **haddock loins**, about
    4 oz each
2 tablespoons **olive oil**
2 teaspoons finely grated
    lemon zest
1 teaspoon **fennel seeds**
6 small **tomatoes**, halved
2 **garlic cloves**, chopped
1 teaspoon **dried oregano**
2 tablespoons **balsamic
    vinegar**
1½ lb **new potatoes**
olive oil spray
salt and **pepper**
oregano leaves, to garnish

Rub the haddock loins with 1 tablespoon of the oil, the lemon zest and fennel seeds. Place in a roasting pan, sprinkle with a little salt and pepper, and allow to marinate in the refrigerator.

Put the tomatoes, cut side up, in one close-fitting layer in a roasting pan. Sprinkle with the garlic, dried oregano, and salt and pepper. Drizzle with the balsamic vinegar and remaining oil and place in a preheated oven, 350°F, for 45 minutes.

Meanwhile, cook the potatoes in a large saucepan of salted boiling water for 18–20 minutes or until tender. Drain, crush lightly with the back of a fork, and tip into an ovenproof dish. Spray with a little olive oil and season.

Remove the tomatoes from the oven and keep warm. Increase the oven temperature to 425°F. Place the potatoes and the haddock loins in the oven for 10–15 minutes or until the fish flakes easily when pressed in the center with a knife and the potatoes are slightly crispy. Serve the fish with the potatoes and tomatoes, garnished with oregano leaves.

For warm smoked haddock salad, replace the haddock loins with 4 smoked haddock fillets. Roast the fish as above, then break into large flakes. Cook the potatoes in a saucepan of boiling water as above, then cut into thick slices. Mix together 1 tablespoon whole grain mustard, 1 teaspoon tarragon vinegar, and 2 tablespoons low-fat sour cream in a bowl. Season, then stir in the potatoes. Pile washed watercress onto serving plates and spoon over the dressed potatoes. Sprinkle with the flaked haddock and serve.

sea bream & red mullet tagine

Serves **4**
Preparation time **15 minutes**
Cooking time **35–40 minutes**

8 oz **sea bream fillets**, cut
   into large chunks
8 oz **red mullet fillets**, cut
   into large chunks
5½ tablespoons **chermoula**
   (see below for homemade)
1 tablespoon **olive oil**
1 **onion**, chopped
1 **celery stick**, chopped
1 **yellow bell pepper**, cored,
   seeded, and sliced
1½ **preserved lemons**,
   chopped
15 **cherry tomatoes**
13 oz can **chickpeas**, drained
pinch of **saffron threads**
1 cup **fish** or **vegetable stock**
16 large, **pitted green olives**
salt and **pepper**
small handful of **cilantro**
   leaves, to garnish

Mix together the fish fillets and 2½ tablespoons of the chermoula in a nonmetallic bowl, cover, and allow to marinate in the refrigerator.

Heat the oil in a large, heavy saucepan over a medium heat, add the onion, celery, and yellow pepper and cook gently for 12–15 minutes or until softened.

Add the preserved lemons, reserving 2 tablespoons for garnish. Stir in the cherry tomatoes, chickpeas, saffron, and remaining chermoula and season to taste with salt and pepper. Stir-fry for 2–3 minutes and then pour over the stock. Bring to a boil, cover, and simmer gently for 10 minutes.

Use a large spoon to remove half of the chickpea mixture from the pan. Lay the marinated fish over the remaining mixture in the pan, then return the chickpeas to the pan, covering the fish. Top with the olives, cover, and simmer gently over a medium-low heat for 10 minutes or until the fish is cooked through.

Ladle the tagine into bowls and sprinkle with the reserved chopped lemon and cilantro leaves. Serve with steamed whole-wheat couscous.

For homemade chermoula, dry-fry 1 teaspoon each of cumin and coriander seeds in a skillet until fragrant, tip into a spice grinder or mini chopper and grind to a powder. Add 1 teaspoon each of ground turmeric and ras el hanout, 2 roughly chopped garlic cloves, 1 small bunch each of parsley and cilantro, and 3 tablespoons lemon juice. Blend until smooth, then stir in 2 tablespoons olive oil. Store in an airtight container in the refrigerator for up to 2–3 days.

red fish curry

Serves **4**
Preparation time **15 minutes**
Cooking time **about
 10 minutes**

1 tablespoon **peanut oil**
1½–2 tablespoons **red
 curry paste** (see below
 for homemade)
¾ cup **coconut cream**
1 cup **vegetable stock**
1 tablespoon **tamarind paste**
1 tablespoon **Thai fish sauce**
1 tablespoon **dark brown
 sugar**
1 cup **broccoli florets**
2 cups **green beans**, trimmed
 and cut into **1** inch lengths
1 lb thick **white fish fillets**,
 skinned, boned, and cut into
 chunks
5 oz can **bamboo shoots**,
 drained (optional)
small handful of **Thai basil** or
 cilantro leaves, to garnish
lime wedges, to serve

Heat the oil in a wok or large skillet over a medium heat, add the curry paste, and stir-fry for 1–2 minutes. Stir in the coconut cream, stock, tamarind paste, fish sauce, and sugar and bring to a boil, then reduce the heat and simmer gently for another 2–3 minutes. Add the broccoli and beans and simmer gently for 2 minutes.

Stir in the fish and simmer gently for an additional 3–4 minutes or until just cooked through. Stir in the bamboo shoots, if using.

Ladle into bowls, sprinkle with the Thai basil or cilantro leaves, and serve with lime wedges and boiled Thai brown rice.

For homemade red curry paste, put 2 roughly chopped garlic cloves, 2 roughly chopped shallots, 2–3 seeded and roughly chopped red chilies, 1 inch piece of peeled and roughly chopped fresh ginger root, 1 chopped lemon grass stalk, 1 tablespoon Thai fish sauce, 1½ tablespoons palm sugar or light brown sugar, 3 shredded kaffir lime leaves or finely grated zest of 1 lime, 1 tablespoon lime juice, ½ teaspoon cumin seeds, and ½ teaspoon coriander seeds in a small food processor and blend to a smooth paste. Store in an airtight container in the refrigerator for up to 1 week.

spicy tuna, tomato, & olive pasta

Serves **4**
Preparation time **10 minutes**
Cooking time **10–12 minutes**

13 oz **penne** or **rigatoni**
2 tablespoons **olive oil**, plus
   extra to serve
2 **garlic cloves**, thinly sliced
large pinch of **red pepper
   flakes**
13 oz **tomatoes**, roughly
   chopped
1/3 cup **pitted black olives**,
   roughly chopped
1 tablespoon roughly chopped
   thyme
10 oz can **tuna** in olive oil,
   drained
salt and **pepper**

Cook the pasta in a large saucepan of salted boiling water for 10–12 minutes, or according to the package instructions, until al dente.

Meanwhile, heat the oil in a large skillet over a medium heat and add the garlic, red pepper flakes, tomatoes, olives, and thyme. Bring to a boil, then reduce the heat and simmer for 5 minutes. Break the tuna up with a fork and stir into the sauce. Simmer for 2 minutes, then season with salt and pepper.

Drain the pasta, then toss into the sauce. Serve immediately, drizzled with extra olive oil.

For fresh tuna sauce, cut a 10 oz tuna steak into strips and season with salt and pepper. Pan-fry in the olive oil for 2 minutes before adding the other ingredients and cooking for 5 minutes.

tuna steaks with wasabi dressing

Serves **4**
Preparation time **5 minutes**
Cooking time **6–7 minutes**

4 **tuna steaks**, about 5 oz
   each
2 teaspoons **mixed
   peppercorns**, crushed
8 oz **sugar snap peas**
1 teaspoon **toasted sesame
   oil**
2 teaspoons **sesame seeds**,
   lightly toasted

Dressing
2 tablespoons **light soy sauce**
4 tablespoons **mirin**
1 teaspoon **sugar**
1 teaspoon **wasabi paste**

Season the tuna steaks with the crushed peppercorns. Heat a griddle pan over a medium-high heat and griddle the tuna steaks for 2 minutes on each side until browned but still pink in the center. Remove from the pan and allow to rest.

Put the sugar snap peas in a steamer basket and lower into a shallow saucepan of boiling water so that the peas are not quite touching the water. Drizzle with the sesame oil, cover, and steam for 2–3 minutes or until tender. Alternatively, cook the peas in a bamboo or electric steamer.

Place all of the dressing ingredients in a screw-top jar and seal with a tight-fitting lid. Shake vigorously until well combined.

Divide the sugar snap peas between 4 serving dishes, then cut the tuna steaks in half diagonally and arrange over the peas. Drizzle with the prepared dressing and sprinkle with the sesame seeds. Serve immediately, with cellophane rice noodles, if desired.

For tuna carpaccio, roll 1 lb tuna fillet in the peppercorns and seal on all sides in a very hot skillet. Cool, wrap in plastic wrap and place in the freezer for 1 hour until semi-frozen. Remove and cut into very thin slices. Arrange the slices on large plates and drizzle with the dressing. Serve with the steamed and chilled sugar snap peas, sprinkle with sesame seeds.

pot-roasted tuna with lentils

Serves **4**

Preparation time **15 minutes**

Cooking time **50 minutes–1 hour 10 minutes**

½ teaspoon **celery salt**

1½ lb **tuna**, in one slender piece

3 tablespoons **olive oil**

1 **fennel bulb**, thinly sliced

1¼ cups **black lentils**, rinsed

1 glass **white wine**, about ⅔ cup

1 cup **fish** or **vegetable stock**

4 tablespoons chopped **fennel leaves** or **dill weed**

2 tablespoons **capers**, rinsed and drained

13 oz can **chopped tomatoes**

salt and **pepper**

Mix the celery salt with a little pepper and rub all over the tuna. Heat the oil in a flameproof casserole over a medium-high heat and fry the tuna on all sides until browned. Remove with a slotted spoon and drain on paper towels on a plate. Add the sliced fennel to the pan and fry gently until softened.

Stir in the lentils and wine and bring to a boil, then cook until the wine has reduced by about half. Stir in the stock, fennel leaves or dill, capers and tomatoes and bring to a boil. Cover and transfer to a preheated oven, 350°F, and cook for 15 minutes.

Add the tuna, return to the oven, and cook for an additional 20 minutes or until the lentils are completely tender and the tuna is still slightly pink in the center. If you prefer it well done, return to the oven for another 15–20 minutes. Season to taste with salt and pepper and serve.

For pot-roasted lamb with lentils, replace the tuna with a 1¼ lb piece of rolled loin of lamb. Omit the fennel bulb and celery salt and fry the lamb in the oil as above. Cook the lentils as above, replacing the fish or vegetable stock with 1 cup chicken stock and the fennel leaves or dill weed with 4 tablespoons chopped rosemary or oregano. Add the lamb and return to the oven for an additional 30 minutes. If you prefer your lamb well done, cook for another 20 minutes.

spicy angler fish & potato bake

Serves **4**
Preparation time **15 minutes**
Cooking time **about 1 hour
   10 minutes**

2 tablespoons **olive oil**
1 large **red onion**, finely sliced
2 **garlic cloves**, 1 chopped
   and 1 crushed
1 teaspoon **turmeric**
1 teaspoon **hot smoked
   paprika**
1 teaspoon **ground cumin**
½ teaspoon **ground ginger**
2 tablespoons **tomato paste**
1 tablespoon **lemon juice**
1¾ lb large **potatoes**, peeled
   and thinly sliced
1 lb **angler fish tail**,
   cut into 4 pieces
8 oz **roasted peppers**, thinly
   sliced
1 **preserved lemon**, finely
   chopped
1¾ cups hot **fish** or **vegetable
   stock**
½ teaspoon **powdered
   saffron**
salt and **pepper**

Heat 1 tablespoon of the oil in a small skillet over a medium heat, add the onion and chopped garlic and fry gently for 10 minutes or until softened.

Meanwhile, mix together all the spices with a little salt and pepper, the tomato paste, lemon juice, crushed garlic, and remaining oil in a nonmetallic dish. Put the potatoes in a large bowl and add all but 1½ tablespoons of the paste. Mix together to coat the potatoes. Rub the remaining paste over the angler fish, cover, and allow to marinate in the refrigerator.

Stir the cooked onion, peppers, and preserved lemon into the potatoes and tip into a large, shallow ovenproof dish. Pour over enough stock to almost cover the potatoes and place in a preheated oven, 350°F, for 45 minutes or until the potatoes are almost tender.

Arrange the angler fish over the potatoes, adding a little more stock if necessary. Sprinkle with the saffron and return to the oven for an additional 10–15 minutes or until the fish is just cooked through. Serve immediately.

For Malaysian-style angler fish, cook 2 tablespoons red curry paste in 1 tablespoon peanut oil in a large skillet. Add the onion and cook for about 5 minutes. Stir in 3 shredded kaffir lime leaves, ¾ cup reduced-fat coconut milk, ¾ cup fish or vegetable stock, 1 tablespoon fish sauce, and 1 tablespoon light soy sauce. Bring to a boil, then tip into a shallow ovenproof dish with 1 lb cubed angler fish tail and bake in the oven for 20 minutes or until the fish is cooked through. Serve with steamed rice.

angler fish & sweet potato curry

Serves **4**
Preparation time **15 minutes**
Cooking time **about
  20 minutes**

2 **lemon grass stalks**, roughly
  chopped
2 **shallots**, roughly chopped
1 large **red chili**, seeded
1 **garlic clove**
¾ inch piece of **fresh ginger
  root**, peeled and chopped
3 tablespoons **peanut oil**
2 x 14 fl oz cans **reduced-fat
  coconut milk**
2 **sweet potatoes**, cut into
  ¾ inch cubes
2 large **angler fish tails**, about
  8 oz each, cut into large
  chunks
2 tablespoons **Thai fish sauce**
1 teaspoon **dark brown sugar**
1½ tablespoons **lime juice**
2 tablespoons roughly
  chopped **cilantro**, to garnish

Put the lemon grass, shallots, chili, garlic, ginger, and
oil in a food processor or blender and blend to a
smooth paste.

Heat a saucepan over a medium heat, add the paste
and fry for 2 minutes until fragrant, then add the
coconut milk. Bring to a boil and cook for 5 minutes
until it reaches the consistency of cream. Add the sweet
potatoes and cook until almost tender.

Add the angler fish and simmer for an additional
5 minutes or until the fish is firm and cooked through.
Add the fish sauce, sugar, and lime juice, to taste.
Sprinkle with the cilantro and serve with some Thai
sticky rice.

**For Thai-roasted angler fish with roasted chili
pumpkin**, mix 2 tablespoons Thai red curry paste with
4 tablespoons fat-free plain yogurt in a nonmetallic
bowl. Add 2 angler fish tails, cut into large pieces,
cover, and allow to marinate in the refrigerator for
at least 20 minutes or overnight if possible. Pan-fry
the pieces of fish in a little vegetable oil until cooked
through. Cut a 1 lb pumpkin in half, scoop out the
seeds, peel, and cut into 1 inch cubes. Sprinkle with
dried red pepper flakes and roast in a preheated oven,
400°F, for 15–20 minutes, or until tender, turning
occasionally. Serve with extra plain yogurt mixed with
chopped cilantro.

angler fish with winter vegetables

Serves **4**
Preparation time **20 minutes**
Cooking time **about**
  40 minutes

2 tablespoons **olive oil**
2 tablespoons **butter**
1 **red onion**, chopped
2 **garlic cloves**, chopped
2¼ cups diced **parsnips**
2½ cups diced **rutabagas**
2½ cups diced **turnips**
2 cups diced **carrots**
1 teaspoon chopped **thyme**
1 tablespoon chopped **sage**
1 teaspoon chopped **dill weed**
1 tablespoon chopped
  oregano or 1 teaspoon
  dried oregano
2 **bay leaves**
1 lb **angler fish tail**, cubed
²/₃ cup **white wine**
²/₃ cup **vegetable stock**
salt and **pepper**

Heat the oil and butter in a large, heavy saucepan over a medium heat, add the onion and garlic and fry for 8–9 minutes or until softened and lightly golden. Add the remaining vegetables and the herbs and stir for 10 minutes or until lightly golden. Remove with a slotted spoon and set aside.

Increase the heat to medium-high, add the fish and season with salt and pepper. Fry for 3–4 minutes, stirring occasionally, or until lightly browned all over. It may be necessary to add an extra teaspoon of oil.

Return the vegetables to the pan, then pour over the wine and stock and stir gently. Bring to a boil, then reduce the heat, cover, and simmer gently for 8–10 minutes or until the fish is cooked through and the vegetables are tender. Serve with steamed curly kale and crusty brown bread.

For angler fish in red wine, make as above, replacing the dill with 1 tablespoon chopped rosemary and the white wine and vegetable stock with 1¼ cups red wine and a 13 oz can chopped tomatoes.

angler fish with coconut rice

Serves **4**
Preparation time **20 minutes**
Cooking time **25–30 minutes**

4 long, slender **lemon grass stalks**

1 ¼ lb **angler fish fillets**, cut into 1 ¼ inch cubes

3 tablespoons **stir-fry** or **wok oil**

½ teaspoon **dried red pepper flakes**

2 **garlic cloves**, sliced

1 bunch of **scallions**, finely chopped, white and green parts separate

1 ½ cups **Thai fragrant rice**

1 ¾ cups can **reduced-fat coconut milk**

2 oz **creamed coconut**, chopped

¾ cup **hot water**

2 tablespoons **rice wine vinegar**

3 cups **baby leaf spinach**

salt and **pepper**

Using a large knife, slice each lemon grass stalk in half lengthwise. (If the stalks are very thick, pull off the outer layers, finely chop them, and add to the oil with the red pepper flakes.) Cut the thin ends of each stalk to a point and thread the angler fish onto the skewers. If it is difficult to thread the fish, pierce each piece with a small knife first to make threading easier.

Heat the oil with the red pepper flakes, garlic, and white parts of the scallions in a large skillet over a medium heat. Add the angler fish skewers and fry gently for about 5 minutes, turning once, until cooked through. Remove from the pan, drain on a plate, and keep warm.

Add the rice, coconut milk, and creamed coconut to the pan, season with salt and pepper to taste, and bring to a boil. Reduce the heat, cover with a lid or foil, and cook gently for 6–8 minutes, stirring frequently, until the rice is almost tender and the milk absorbed. Add the measurement water and cook, covered, for an additional 10 minutes or until the rice is completely tender, adding a little more water if the mixture boils dry before the rice is tender.

Stir in the vinegar, remaining scallions, and spinach, turning it in the rice until wilted. Arrange the skewers over the rice. Cover and cook gently for 3 minutes, then serve immediately.

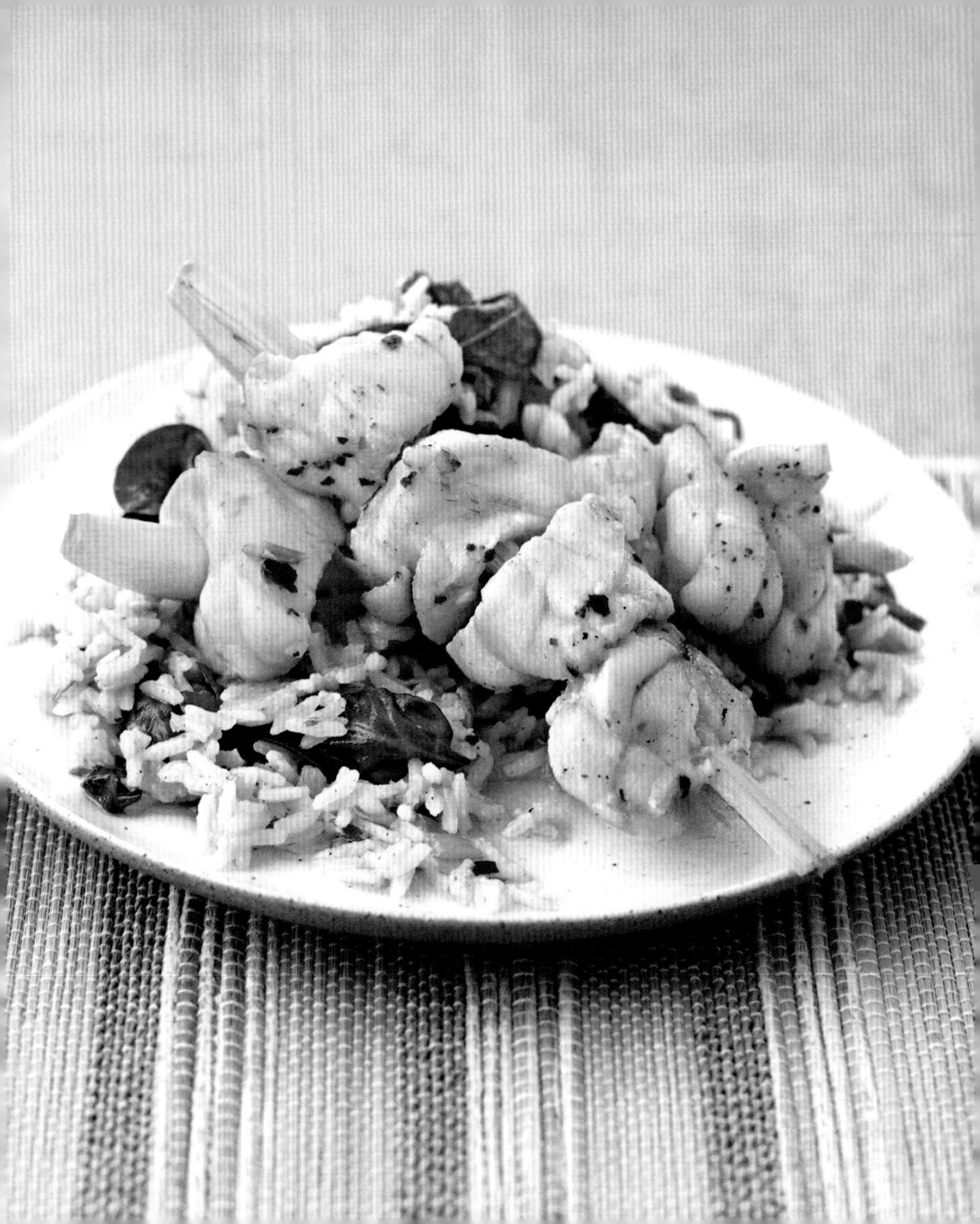

poached sea bass & salsa

Serves **4**
Preparation time **15 minutes**
Cooking time **25 minutes**

2 inch piece of **fresh ginger
root**, peeled and thinly sliced
2 **lemon grass stalks**, sliced
lengthwise
1 **lime**, sliced
¾ cup **dry sherry**
2 tablespoons **fish sauce**
2 **sea bass**, about 1¼ lb each,
cleaned and scaled

Salsa
3 firm **tomatoes**, seeded and
finely diced
1 **lemon grass stalk**, tough
outer leaves discarded, finely
chopped
1 teaspoon peeled and finely
grated **fresh ginger root**
2 tablespoons chopped
cilantro
2 **scallions**, finely chopped
2 teaspoons **peanut oil**
1 tablespoon **lime juice**
1½ teaspoons **light soy
sauce**

Put the ginger, lemon grass, lime, sherry, fish sauce, and enough water to just cover the fish in a fish poacher or large skillet. Bring to a boil, then reduce the heat and simmer gently for 5 minutes.

Place the sea bass in the fish poacher or on a large piece of nonstick parchment paper if using a skillet. Lower into the stock, adding more water if necessary so that it covers the fish. Bring the stock to a boil and then turn off the heat. Cover and allow to poach for 15 minutes or until the fish flakes easily when pressed in the center with a knife.

Meanwhile, make the salsa. Place the tomatoes, lemon grass, ginger, cilantro, and scallions in a bowl. Stir through the oil, lime juice, and soy sauce and allow to infuse.

Lift the poached sea bass carefully from the cooking liquid onto a plate. Peel away the skin and gently lift the fillets from the bones. Place on a serving dish with the salsa and serve with steamed rice and lime wedges, if desired.

For pan-fried sea bass with salsa, ask the fish merchant to fillet the whole sea bass. Heat 1 tablespoon olive oil in a nonstick skillet and pan-fry the sea bass fillets over a medium-high heat, skin side down, for 3–4 minutes. Reduce the heat, cover, and cook for an additional 3–4 minutes or until cooked through. Serve with the salsa.

flounder with vegetables provençale

Serves **4**

Preparation time **15 minutes**

Cooking time **45–50 minutes**

2 **zucchini**, sliced

1 **eggplant**, sliced

4 **tomatoes**, quartered

1 **onion**, thickly sliced

1 large **red bell pepper**,
  cored, seeded, and sliced

3 **garlic cloves**, sliced

1 small bunch of **basil**,
  chopped, plus extra
  shredded leaves to garnish

1 tablespoon chopped **thyme**

3 tablespoons chopped
  parsley

olive oil spray

3 tablespoons **all-purpose
  flour**

4 **flounder fillets**, about 5 oz
  each

1½ tablespoons **olive oil**

salt and **pepper**

Mix all the vegetables and the chopped herbs in a large roasting pan and season with salt and pepper. Spray with a little olive oil and place in a preheated oven, 350°F, for 40–45 minutes or until the vegetables are tender.

Put the flour on a plate and season with salt and pepper, then dust the fish fillets in the flour. Heat the oil in a large, nonstick skillet over a medium heat, add the fish, skin side down, and fry for 2–3 minutes, then turn the fish over using a spatula and cook for an additional 2–3 minutes or until golden. The flesh should be white and flake easily when pressed in the center with a knife.

Spoon the vegetables onto serving plates and top with the fish fillets. Serve immediately, garnished with the shredded basil.

For vegetable provençale bake, slice all the vegetables and arrange in a shallow ovenproof dish. Season with salt and pepper, drizzle with the olive oil, and pour over 2 cups pureed tomatoes. Sprinkle with the chopped herbs and 2 tablespoons grated Parmesan cheese. Place in the preheated oven for 45 minutes or until the vegetables are tender. Serve with a green salad and crusty bread.

feta-stuffed flounder

Serves **4**
Preparation time **20 minutes**
Cooking time **40 minutes**

2 tablespoons chopped **mint**
2 tablespoons chopped
  oregano
1 oz **prosciutto**, finely
  chopped
2 **garlic cloves**, finely chopped
4 **scallions**, finely chopped
7 oz **reduced-fat feta cheese**
8 **flounder fillets**, skinned
2 **zucchini**, sliced
4 tablespoons **garlic-infused**
  olive oil
8 **flat mushrooms**
5 oz **baby plum tomatoes**,
  halved
1 tablespoon **capers**, rinsed
  and drained
salt and **pepper**

Put the mint, oregano, prosciutto, garlic, and scallions in a bowl. Crumble in the feta cheese, season with plenty of pepper, and mix together well.

Put the fish fillets, skin side up, on a clean work surface and press the feta mixture down the centers. Roll up loosely and secure with wooden toothpicks.

Arrange the zucchini in a shallow, ovenproof dish and drizzle with 1 tablespoon of the oil. Place in a preheated oven, 375°F, for 15 minutes. Add the fish fillets to the dish. Tuck the mushrooms, tomatoes, and capers around the fish and season lightly with salt and pepper. Drizzle with the remaining oil.

Return to the oven for an additional 25 minutes or until the fish is cooked through. Serve with tomato and garlic bread (see below).

For tomato & garlic bread, to serve as an accompaniment, mix together 6 tablespoons softened butter, 2 crushed garlic cloves, 3 tablespoons sundried tomato paste, and a little salt and pepper. Make vertical cuts 1 inch apart through a ciabatta loaf, cutting not quite through the base. Push the garlic and tomato paste mixture into the cuts. Wrap in foil and bake in the oven on the shelf beneath the fish for 15 minutes, then open up the foil and return the bread to the oven for 10 minutes.

pollack with puy lentils & fennel

Serves **4**

Preparation time **12 minutes**

Cooking time **about 25 minutes**

2 **fennel bulbs,** thinly sliced

7 cups **vegetable stock**

1 ¼ cups **Puy lentils,** rinsed

1 ½ tablespoons **olive oil**

1 **onion,** chopped

1 **garlic clove,** chopped

1 cup **sundried tomatoes** (not in oil), chopped

1 small bunch of **parsley,** chopped, plus extra to garnish

finely grated zest and juice of 1 lemon

4 thick **pollack fillets,** about 5 oz each

2 teaspoons **capers,** rinsed, drained, and chopped

4 large, slices of lean **prosciutto ham**

salt and **pepper**

Arrange the fennel over the base of a large ovenproof dish. Pour over ¾ cup of the stock to just cover the slices. Season with salt and pepper and place in a preheated oven, 350°F, for about 25 minutes or until softened.

Meanwhile, put the remaining stock and lentils in a large saucepan and bring to a boil. Reduce the heat and simmer for 20 minutes or until tender. Drain the lentils, reserving ¾ cup of the cooking liquid.

Heat 1 tablespoon of the oil in another saucepan over a medium heat, add the onion and fry for 7−8 minutes or until softened. Add the garlic and cook for an additional 2−3 minutes. Stir the drained lentils into the onions with the reserved cooking liquid and the sundried tomatoes and simmer for 1−2 minutes. Stir in the parsley and lemon juice and season to taste.

Towards the end of the fennel and lentil cooking time, sprinkle each pollack fillet with a little of the lemon zest and capers. Season with pepper, then wrap each fillet in a slice of prosciutto. Heat the remaining oil in a large, nonstick skillet over a medium-high heat, add the pollack fillets, and cook for 6−8 minutes, turning occasionally, until the fish is cooked through and the prosciutto crisp. Remove from the pan, drain on paper towels, and rest for 2−3 minutes.

Spoon the lentils into dishes and top with the fennel. Slice the fish in half diagonally and arrange over the fennel. Serve immediately with extra chopped parsley sprinkled over.

clam & tomato spaghetti

Serves **4**
Preparation time **10 minutes**
Cooking time **20–25 minutes**

2 tablespoons **olive oil**
1 **onion**, sliced
2 **garlic cloves**, finely chopped
1 **red chili**, seeded and finely
   chopped (optional)
15 **cherry tomatoes**,
   quartered
½ cup **dry white wine**
2–3 tablespoons chopped
   parsley
2 lb **live clams**, cleaned
   (discard any that don't shut
   when tapped)
13 oz **whole-wheat spaghetti**
1½ tablespoons **truffle oil**
salt and **pepper**

Heat the olive oil in a large saucepan over a low heat, add the onion and garlic and cook for 12–15 minutes or until softened. Add the chili, if using, tomatoes, white wine, and parsley and season with salt and pepper. Bring to a boil, then reduce the heat and simmer for 2–3 minutes.

Add the clams, cover with a tight-fitting lid, and cook gently for 4–5 minutes or until they have opened. Discard any clams that remain closed.

Meanwhile, cook the spaghetti in a large saucepan of salted boiling water for 10–12 minutes, or according to the package instructions, until al dente. Drain well and place in a serving dish.

Heap the clam and tomato sauce over the spaghetti, drizzle with the truffle oil, and sprinkle with pepper. Serve immediately with crusty bread.

For mixed seafood fettucine, replace the spaghetti with 13 oz fettucine and cook the pasta as above. Make the tomato sauce as above, allowing it to simmer for 10 minutes after adding the wine. Omit the live clams and stir through 13 oz raw peeled fruits de mer or seafood selection, and cook for 5 minutes or until the seafood is cooked through and piping hot. Serve with the fettucine as above, drizzled with basil or chili oil.

scallops with spiced lentils

Serves **4**
Preparation time **10 minutes**
Cooking time **20–25 minutes**

1 1/4 cups **red lentils**, rinsed
5 tablespoons **olive oil**
2 tablespoons **butter**
1 **onion**, finely chopped
1 **eggplant**, cut into 1/2 inch
  cubes
1 **garlic clove**, finely chopped
1 tablespoon **curry powder**
1 tablespoon chopped
  parsley, plus extra to garnish
12 cleaned **sea scallops**,
  corals removed (optional)
4 tablespoons **fat-free plain
  yogurt**
salt and **pepper**

Cook the lentils in a saucepan of boiling water according to the package instructions. Drain well.

Meanwhile, heat 1 tablespoon of the oil and the butter in a skillet over a medium heat, add the onion and cook slowly for 10 minutes or until golden brown. Remove with a slotted spoon to a plate and turn the heat up to high. Add another 2 tablespoons of the oil to the pan and fry the eggplant in batches until browned and softened.

Return the onion to the pan with the garlic, curry powder, and cooked lentils and fry for another minute to warm through. Season with salt and pepper and stir in the parsley.

Heat a skillet over a high heat, then add the remaining 2 tablespoons of oil. Season the scallops with salt and pepper, place them in the skillet, and cook for 1 minute on each side or until just cooked through. Serve the scallops immediately with the spiced lentils and yogurt, garnished with parsley leaves.

For scallops with dhal & spinach, cook 1 1/4 cups yellow split pea lentils according to the package instructions and drain well. Heat a little vegetable oil in a skillet, add the onion and garlic, omitting the eggplant, and fry until softened. Add 1 teaspoon curry powder, 1 teaspoon garam masala, and a pinch of turmeric and fry for 1 minute. Add the cooked lentils with a little water or chicken stock to moisten the mixture. Add 1 lb baby leaf spinach and stir until wilted. Cook the scallops as above with a light sprinkle of curry powder on each. Serve with the dhal.

shrimp & soba noodle salad

Serves **4**

Preparation time **10 minutes**,
plus cooling

Cooking time **about
10 minutes**

13 oz **raw peeled shrimp**
finely grated zest of **1 lime**
1 tablespoon peeled and finely
shredded **fresh ginger root**
1 **red chili**, seeded and finely
chopped
13 oz **soba noodles**
2 **scallions**, thinly sliced

Dressing
juice of **1 lime**
1 tablespoon **dark brown
sugar**
2 tablespoons **mirin**
2 tablespoons **fish sauce**
1 small bunch of **cilantro**,
chopped
1 small bunch of **mint**,
chopped

Mix together the shrimp, lime zest, ginger, and chili in a bowl. Tip into a steamer basket and lower into a shallow saucepan of boiling water so the shrimp are not quite touching the water. Cover and steam for 3–4 minutes or until the shrimp turn pink and are cooked through. Alternatively, cook the shrimp in a bamboo or electric steamer. Remove from the pan and allow to cool.

Meanwhile, beat together all the dressing ingredients in a small bowl.

Cook the noodles in a large saucepan of boiling water for 6–7 minutes, or according to the package instructions, until tender. Drain well and rinse under running cold water. Toss with the dressing.

Divide the noodles between 4 bowls, sprinkle over the scallions and shrimp and serve immediately.

For aromatic shrimp stir-fry, heat 2 teaspoons peanut oil in a hot wok or large skillet and stir-fry the marinated shrimp until they turn pink and are just cooked through. Add the drained noodles and toss to reheat. Drizzle over the dressing and serve immediately, sprinkled with the scallions.

mussels with bacon

Serves **4**
Preparation time **8 minutes**
Cooking time **30–35 minutes**

6 lean **Canadian bacon
  slices**, chopped
2 **shallots**, sliced
2 **garlic cloves**, chopped
1 cup **white wine**
13 oz can **chopped tomatoes**
1 tablespoon chopped **thyme**,
  plus extra sprigs to garnish
4 lb **live mussels**, scrubbed
  and debearded (discard any
  that don't shut when tapped)
2–3 tablespoons **low-fat sour
  cream** (optional)
salt and **pepper**

Heat a very large, heavy saucepan over a medium heat, then add the bacon and dry-fry for 3–4 minutes or until beginning to brown. If the bacon is very lean, fry in 1 tablespoon olive oil. Add the shallots and garlic and fry for 2–3 minutes or until softened.

Stir in the white wine, tomatoes, and thyme and season with salt and pepper to taste. Bring to a boil, then reduce the heat and simmer for 20 minutes or until the sauce has thickened.

Add the mussels and stir to coat, then cover with a tight-fitting lid and cook for 4–5 minutes, or until the mussels have opened, stirring once. Discard any that remain closed.

Stir in the sour cream, if using, and serve in deep bowls garnished with thyme sprigs.

For traditional moules marinières, omit the bacon and cook the shallots and garlic in a knob of butter. Pour in the white wine, or replace with 1 cup hard cider, and then add the mussels. Cook as above. Stir in the sour cream and sprinkle with chopped parsley to serve.

peanut, squid, & noodle salad

Serves **4**
Preparation time **25 minutes**,
  plus standing
Cooking time **15 minutes**

6 oz **thin rice noodles**
1 lb prepared **baby squid**,
  cleaned
3 **red chilies**, seeded and
  finely chopped
3 **garlic cloves**, finely chopped
2 tablespoons chopped
  cilantro, plus extra leaves to
  garnish
3 tablespoons **peanut oil**
¾ cup **unsalted peanuts**,
  roughly chopped
1 cup **green beans**, trimmed
  and shredded
3 tablespoons **Thai fish sauce**
1 teaspoon **superfine sugar**
3 tablespoons **lemon juice**
lime wedges, to serve
  (optional)

Put the noodles in a large heatproof bowl, pour over boiling water to cover, and allow to stand for 5–8 minutes, or according to the package instructions, until tender. Drain well and rinse in cold water.

Cut the squid bodies in half lengthwise and use a sharp knife to make a series of slashes in a diagonal criss-cross pattern on the underside of each piece.

Mix together the chilies, garlic, and chopped cilantro in a nonmetallic bowl. Add the squid pieces and toss in the mixture, then allow to stand for about 20 minutes.

Heat the oil in a wok or large skillet over a medium heat and toast the peanuts for 2–3 minutes or until golden brown. Remove with a slotted spoon and set aside. Add the squid to the wok or pan and stir-fry for 2–3 minutes or until the squid have begun to curl and turn white. Set aside with the peanuts.

Add the beans to the wok or pan and stir-fry for 2 minutes. Stir in the fish sauce, sugar, lemon juice, and 3 tablespoons water and cook for another 1 minute. Remove the pan from the heat, add the drained noodles and toss together. Add the peanuts, squid, and extra cilantro leaves and toss again. Serve warm or cool with lime wedges, if desired.

meat &
poultry

gingery pork chops

Serves **4**
Preparation time **15 minutes**
Cooking time **20 minutes**

4 lean **pork chops**, about
   5 oz each
1½ inch piece of **fresh ginger
   root**, peeled and grated
1 teaspoon **sesame oil**
1 tablespoon **dark soy sauce**
2 teaspoons **stem ginger
   syrup** or **honey**

Dressing
1½ tablespoons **light soy
   sauce**
juice of 1 **blood orange**
2 pieces of **stem ginger**, finely
   chopped

Salad
2 large **carrots**, peeled and
   coarsely grated
1¼ cups **snow peas**,
   shredded
1 cup **bean sprouts**
2 **scallions**, thinly sliced
2 tablespoons **unsalted
   peanuts**, roughly chopped
   (optional)

Place the pork in a shallow ovenproof dish and rub with the ginger, sesame oil, soy sauce, and stem ginger syrup or honey until well covered. Allow to marinate for 10 minutes.

Make the dressing. Mix together all the ingredients in a bowl and set aside for the flavors to develop.

Cook the pork in a preheated oven, 350°F, for 18–20 minutes or until cooked through but still juicy.

Meanwhile, mix the carrots, snow peas, bean sprouts, and scallions in a large bowl. Just before serving, toss with the dressing and pile into serving dishes. Sprinkle with the peanuts, if using, and top with the pork chops, drizzled with cooking juices. Serve immediately with steamed rice.

For pork & ginger stir-fry, replace the pork chops with 4 lean boneless pork loin steaks and thinly slice. Cut the carrots into matchsticks. Heat 1–2 teaspoons sesame oil in a hot wok or large skillet, add the pork and stir-fry until just cooked. Add the carrots, snow peas, bean sprouts, and scallions and stir-fry for another 1–2 minutes. Toss with the dressing and serve immediately, sprinkled with the peanuts, if desired.

soy & sake pork with bok choy

Serves **4**
Preparation time **5 minutes**
Cooking time **15–20 minutes**

6 tablespoons **Japanese soy sauce**
6 tablespoons **sake**
1½ tablespoons **sugar**
1 lb lean **pork loin** or **tenderloin**, cut into 1 inch cubes
1½ lb **bok choy**, cut in half lengthwise
sesame seeds, to garnish

Put the soy sauce, sake, and sugar in a large, deep skillet and stir to dissolve the sugar. Bring to a boil and simmer for 3–4 minutes. Add the pork and simmer gently for 7–8 minutes, or until the pork is just cooked through, turning occasionally. Remove from the heat and allow to rest.

Place the bok choy in a steamer basket and lower into a shallow saucepan of boiling water so that the bok choy is not quite touching the water. Cover and steam for 3–4 minutes or until tender. Alternatively, use a bamboo or electric steamer.

Arrange the bok choy in serving dishes with the pork and its cooking liquid and steamed Thai jasmine rice. Sprinkle with sesame seeds and serve immediately.

For Japanese tofu & vegetables, make as above, replacing the pork with 1 lb firm, sliced or cubed tofu and the bok choy with 2 cups green beans and 1 lb mixed Asian-style vegetables.

pork & broccoli noodles

Serves **4**

Preparation time **10 minutes**

Cooking time **about 20 minutes**

2 tablespoons **light soy sauce**

1 teaspoon **fish sauce**

2 tablespoons **oyster sauce**

1 lb **pork tenderloin**

1 tablespoon **peanut oil**

2 large **eggs**, lightly beaten

2 **scallions**, finely sliced

13 oz **purple sprouting broccoli spears**

13 oz **thick rice noodles**

Mix together the soy sauce, fish sauce, and oyster sauce in a bowl. Rub half of the sauce over the pork and place in a small, nonstick roasting pan. Place in a preheated oven, 350°F, for about 20 minutes or until cooked through but still juicy. Allow to rest for 5–10 minutes.

Meanwhile, heat the oil in a smoking hot wok or large skillet and pour in the beaten eggs, swirling to cover the hot surface. Sprinkle with the sliced scallions and cook for 1–2 minutes or until the egg is set and beginning to brown. Remove and slice thinly.

Put the broccoli in a steamer basket and lower into a shallow saucepan of boiling water so that the spears are not quite touching the water. Cover and steam for 3–4 minutes or until just tender. Alternatively, use a bamboo or electric steamer.

Cook the noodles in a large saucepan of boiling water for 3–4 minutes, or according to the package instructions, until tender. Drain and heap onto serving plates.

Toss the broccoli in the remaining sauce mixture, spoon onto the noodles and sprinkle with the sliced omelet. Slice the pork and arrange over the noodles. Drizzle with any cooking juices and serve immediately.

For quick pork stir-fry, make the omelet as above and set aside. Reheat the wok or skillet and stir-fry the thinly sliced pork tenderloin until almost cooked through. Add the broccoli spears, cook for another 2–3 minutes, then pour over the sauce. Serve immediately with boiled rice or egg noodles and the sliced omelet.

lamb skewers with turkish salad

Serves **4**
Preparation time **20 minutes**
Cooking time **5–10 minutes**

1 ½ lb boned rib of **lamb**,
  trimmed and cubed
1 teaspoon **olive oil**
1 teaspoon **dried oregano**
finely grated zest of **1 lemon**
½ teaspoon **ground paprika**
4 whole-wheat **pita breads**
salt and **pepper**
lemon wedges, to serve
  (optional)

Turkish salad
1 small **cucumber**, seeded
  and chopped
4 firm, ripe **tomatoes**, seeded
  and chopped
1 **green bell pepper**, cored,
  seeded, and chopped
1 small **red onion**, chopped
1 small bunch of **mint**, finely
  chopped
1 tablespoon **extra virgin
  canola** or **olive oil**
4 oz **reduced-fat feta cheese**,
  diced
2 tablespoons chopped
  parsley
juice of **1 lemon**

Rub the lamb with the olive oil, dried oregano, lemon zest, paprika, and salt and pepper. Thread onto 4 long or 8 short metal skewers and allow to marinate for at least 10 minutes.

Make the salad. Mix together the cucumber, tomatoes, green pepper, onion, mint, and canola or olive oil in a large serving bowl and sprinkle with the feta and parsley. Stir in the lemon juice and season well with salt and pepper. Set aside.

Cook the lamb skewers under a preheated hot broiler or on the barbecue for 5–10 minutes, or until cooked to the pinkness desired, turning occasionally. Remove from the heat and allow to rest for 2–3 minutes.

Meanwhile, wrap the pita breads in foil and place in a preheated oven, 350°F, for 5–8 minutes or until warm. Arrange the lamb skewers on the pita breads with the Turkish salad. Serve with lemon wedges and griddled eggplants, if desired (see below).

For griddled eggplants, to serve as an accompaniment, cut 2 medium eggplants into ¼ inch slices. Preheat a ridged griddle pan over a medium-high heat, add the eggplant slices in batches, and cook for 4–5 minutes, turning once, until charred and tender. Place in a serving dish, season with a little salt and pepper, and drizzle with extra virgin canola oil.

japanese beef noodles

Serves **4**

Preparation time **10 minutes**, plus freezing

Cooking time **8 minutes**

13 oz thin **beef tenderloin**

3 tablespoons **Japanese soy sauce**

3 tablespoons **mirin**

3 tablespoons **sake**

1½ teaspoons **sugar**

13 oz **brown udon noodles**

1 tablespoon **toasted sesame oil**

2 **onions**, sliced

7 oz **shiitake** or **chestnut mushrooms**, sliced

1½ cups **bean sprouts** or **enoki mushrooms**

1 **scallion**, thinly sliced

2 teaspoons **sesame seeds**

Wrap the beef in plastic wrap and place in the freezer for about 1 hour until it is semi-frozen. Remove and use a sharp knife to slice very thinly, against the grain.

Beat together the soy sauce, mirin, sake, and sugar in a small bowl to make a sauce.

Cook the noodles in a large saucepan of boiling water for 6–8 minutes, or according to the package instructions, until tender.

Meanwhile, heat a wok or large skillet until smoking hot, add the sesame oil and onions and stir-fry for 2–3 minutes. Add the shiitake or chestnut mushrooms and the bean sprouts or enoki mushrooms and stir-fry for an additional 2–3 minutes or until softened. Stir in the beef and fry for 2 minutes, then pour in the prepared sauce and bubble for 1 minute.

Drain the noodles and heap into deep bowls, then spoon over the beef, pouring over any sauce left in the wok. Sprinkle with the scallion and sesame seeds and serve immediately.

For tofu, mushroom, & snow pea stir-fry, make the sauce and cook the noodles as above. Replace the beef with 13 oz firm silken tofu, sliced. Stir-fry the onions and mushrooms as above, then add the tofu and 1 cup snow peas and stir-fry for 2–3 minutes. Pour in the sauce and continue as above.

thai-style beef salad

Serves **4–6**
Preparation time **20 minutes**
Cooking time **10 minutes**

4 oz **green papaya**, peeled
  and seeded
4 oz **green mango**, peeled
  and pitted
handful of **mint leaves**,
  chopped
handful of **Thai basil leaves**
2 small, elongated **shallots**,
  finely sliced
1 tablespoon **vegetable oil**
4 **sirloin steaks**, about 4 oz
  each

Dressing
½ inch piece of **fresh ginger
  root**, peeled and finely sliced
1 ½ tablespoons **palm sugar**
  or **light brown sugar**
½ **red chili**, seeded and finely
  sliced
juice of 2 **limes**
2 tablespoons **Thai fish sauce**

Grate or slice the papaya and mango into long, thin strips. Put the papaya and mango, mint and basil leaves in a large salad bowl and mix together, then stir in the shallots.

Make the dressing. Crush the ginger and sugar using a mortar and pestle. Add the chili, lime juice, and fish sauce, to taste.

Heat a griddle pan over a high heat, add the oil and fry the steak for 5 minutes on each side or until cooked to the pinkness desired. Remove from the pan and allow to rest for 5 minutes.

Slice the steak diagonally into thin slices and arrange on serving plates. Add the dressing to the salad, mix well to combine, and serve with the steak.

For toasted rice khao koor, a special garnish you can add to this salad, put 3 tablespoons raw jasmine rice in a small skillet over a medium heat, stirring continuously, until all the rice is golden in color. Allow the rice to cool, then grind it coarsely in a spice grinder or using a mortar and pestle, and sprinkle over the finished salad.

slow-cook beef curry

Serves **4–6**
Preparation time **20 minutes**
Cooking time **2¼ hours**

1 tablespoon **peanut oil**
1 large **onion**, chopped
1½ lb **stewing steak**, cubed
2 tablespoons **tomato paste**
3 **tomatoes**, chopped
3 tablespoons **fat-free plain
  yogurt**, plus extra to serve
1 teaspoon **black onion
  seeds**
salt and **pepper**

Curry paste
2 teaspoons **cumin seeds**
1 teaspoon **coriander seeds**
½ teaspoon **fennel seeds**
2 **garlic cloves**, chopped
1 tablespoon peeled and
  grated **fresh ginger root**
1–2 small **green chilies**,
  according to taste
1 teaspoon **ground paprika**
1 teaspoon **turmeric**
2 tablespoons **tomato paste**
2 tablespoons **peanut oil**
1 cup **cilantro leaves**, plus
  extra to garnish

Make the curry paste. Place the whole spices in a small skillet and dry-fry over a medium heat for 2–3 minutes, stirring frequently, until fragrant and beginning to pop. Grind to a powder in a spice mill or mini chopper. Add to the remaining curry paste ingredients and blend to a smooth paste.

Heat the oil in a large, heavy saucepan over a medium heat, add the onion and cook for 5–6 minutes or until beginning to brown, stirring occasionally. Add 3 tablespoons of the prepared curry paste and stir-fry for 1–2 minutes to cook the spices.

Stir in the beef and cook for 4–5 minutes or until the meat is browned and well coated. Stir in the tomato paste, tomatoes, and 1 cup water. Stir in the yogurt and bring to a boil, then reduce the heat, cover, and simmer very gently for 2 hours or until tender, adding more liquid if necessary. Alternatively, cook in a slow cooker.

Season well with salt and pepper, then ladle into bowls. Spoon over extra yogurt and sprinkle with the black onion seeds and extra cilantro. Serve hot with naan bread and steamed basmati rice, if desired.

For lamb curry with spinach & chickpeas, make the curry as above, replacing the curry paste with 4 tablespoons ready-made madras or rogan josh curry paste and the beef with 1½ lb cubed lean leg of lamb. Stir a drained 13 oz can chickpeas into the curry with the yogurt. Cook as above, stirring in 2½ cups baby leaf spinach at the end of the cooking time. Serve with naan bread and yogurt, if desired.

griddled beef & truffle polenta

Serves **4**
Preparation time **15 minutes**
Cooking time **15–20 minutes**

1 cup **dried porcini
mushrooms**, soaked in
1 cup boiling water for
10–15 minutes
7 teaspoons **olive oil**
1 **garlic clove**, chopped
3 cups **hot beef**
or **vegetable stock**
6 tablespoons chopped
chives
4 **beef tenderloin steaks**,
about 6 oz each
1¼ cups **quick-cook polenta**
½ cup finely grated **Parmesan
cheese**
2 teaspoons **truffle oil**
½ teaspoon **truffle salt**
(optional)
handful of **arugula leaves**
salt and **pepper**

Drain the porcini, reserving the soaking liquid, then squeeze dry and roughly chop. Heat 3 teaspoons of the olive oil in a small skillet over a medium heat, add the garlic and fry for 30 seconds. Add the mushrooms and fry for 1–2 minutes, then stir in 3 tablespoons of the reserved soaking liquid, 3 tablespoons of the stock and 1 tablespoon of the chives. Bubble for 1 minute, then remove from the heat and keep warm.

Rub 1 teaspoon of the remaining olive oil over each of the steaks, season with pepper, and place on a preheated hot griddle pan. Cook for 2–5 minutes on each side until cooked to the pinkness desired. Remove and allow to rest for 4–5 minutes.

Pour the remaining mushroom soaking liquid and stock into a large saucepan and bring to a boil. Pour in the polenta in a steady stream, beating gently until the polenta thickens, then reduce the heat and cook for 2 minutes. Stir in the Parmesan, truffle oil, and 4 tablespoons of the chives. Season to taste.

Spoon the polenta onto serving plates and spoon over the mushrooms and sauce. Slice the steaks in half diagonally and place on top with any cooking juices. Sprinkle with pepper and a scant pinch of truffle salt, if using. Garnish with the remaining chives and serve immediately with griddled zucchini (see below).

For griddled zucchini, to serve as an accompaniment, thinly slice 2 zucchini lengthwise. Heat a ridged griddle pan until very hot. When hot, add the zucchini and cook for 2–3 minutes on each side or until softened and charred.

herby chicken & ricotta cannelloni

Serves **4**
Preparation time **20 minutes**
Cooking time **40–50 minutes**

2 tablespoons **olive oil**
1 lb boneless, skinless
   chicken thighs, finely
   chopped or minced
2 **leeks**, trimmed, cleaned, and
   diced
2 cups **pureed tomatoes**
6 tablespoons chopped mixed
   herbs, such as **parsley,
   chives, sage, marjoram,**
   and **dill weed**
1 teaspoon **fennel seeds**
1 cup **ricotta cheese**
finely grated zest of **1 lemon**
½ teaspoon **ground nutmeg**
1 teaspoon **sweet paprika**
½ cup **frozen chopped
   spinach**, thawed
1 ½ cups **sundried tomatoes**
   (not in oil), chopped
   (optional)
8 oz **cannelloni tubes**
2–3 tablespoons finely grated
   Parmesan cheese
salt and **pepper**

Heat 1 tablespoon of the oil in a large, nonstick skillet over a medium-high heat, add the chicken and fry for 3–4 minutes or until browned, stirring frequently. Reduce the heat slightly, add the leeks and cook for an additional 3–4 minutes or until the leeks are translucent.

Meanwhile, heat the pureed tomatoes in a saucepan and stir in one-third of the chopped herbs, the fennel seeds, and the remaining oil. Season with salt and pepper to taste, then simmer gently for 2–3 minutes.

Remove the chicken from the heat and stir in the ricotta, the remaining chopped herbs, the lemon zest, nutmeg, paprika, spinach, and sundried tomatoes, if using. Season to taste. Stand the cannelloni tubes upright and use a narrow spoon to fill them with the ricotta mixture.

Spoon half of the pureed tomatoes over the base of a large, shallow ovenproof dish. Arrange the filled pasta tubes, side by side over the tomato sauce, so that they all fit in one closely fitting layer. Pour the remaining tomatoes over the top of the cannelloni, then sprinkle with the Parmesan.

Place in a preheated oven, 350°F, for 35–40 minutes or until cooked through and bubbling. Serve hot with a crisp green salad.

For chicken & ricotta lasagna, replace the chicken thighs with 8 oz chopped cooked chicken and omit the leeks. Stir the chicken and fennel seeds into the ricotta mixture as above. Layer lasagna sheets with the chicken mixture and the pureed tomatoes. Sprinkle with Parmesan and cook as above.

chicken & barley risotto

Serves **4**
Preparation time **15 minutes**
Cooking time **about 1 hour**
   10 minutes

2 tablespoons **olive oil**
6 boneless, skinless **chicken thighs**, diced
1 **onion**, roughly chopped
2 **garlic cloves**, finely chopped
7 oz **chestnut mushrooms**, sliced
1 ¼ cups **pearl barley**
¾ cup **red wine**
5 cups **chicken stock**
salt and **pepper**
parsley leaves, to garnish
Parmesan cheese shavings, to serve

Heat the oil in a large skillet over a medium-high heat, add the chicken and onion and fry for 5 minutes, stirring until lightly browned.

Stir in the garlic and mushrooms and fry for 2 minutes, then mix in the pearl barley. Add the red wine, half the stock and season with plenty of salt and pepper, then bring to a boil, stirring continuously. Reduce the heat, cover, and simmer for 1 hour, topping up with extra stock as needed, until the chicken is cooked through and the barley is soft.

Spoon into shallow bowls and garnish with the parsley and sprinkle with Parmesan. Serve with garlic bread and salad, if desired.

For chicken & red rice risotto, fry the chicken and 1 chopped red onion as above. Add the garlic and 7 oz skinned and diced tomatoes, omitting the mushrooms and pearl barley. Stir in 1 ¼ cups red Camargue rice, cook for 1 minute, then add the red wine. Gradually add the hot stock a small ladleful at a time and stirring constantly, only adding more once the rice has absorbed the previous ladleful. Continue until all the liquid has been absorbed and the chicken and rice are tender. This should take about 25 minutes. Crumble 4 oz St Agur or Roquefort cheese on top.

chicken & azuki bean salad

Serves **4**
Preparation time **15 minutes**
Cooking time **2–3 minutes**

1 **green bell pepper**, cored,
    seeded, and chopped
1 **red bell pepper**, cored,
    seeded, and chopped
1 small **red onion**, finely
    chopped
13 oz can **azuki beans**,
    drained
7 oz can **corn**, drained
1 small bunch of **cilantro**,
    chopped
²/₃ cup unsweetened **coconut
    chips** or **flakes**
8 oz cooked **chicken breast**,
    shredded
small handful of **alfalfa shoots**
    (optional)

Dressing
3 tablespoons **light peanut oil**
2 tablespoons **light soy sauce**
2 teaspoons peeled and
    grated **fresh ginger root**
1 tablespoon **rice vinegar**

Mix together the green and red peppers, onion, azuki beans, corn, and half the cilantro in a large bowl. Beat together the dressing ingredients in a separate bowl, then stir 3 tablespoons into the bean salad. Spoon the salad into serving dishes.

Place the coconut chips or flakes in a nonstick skillet over a medium heat and dry-fry for 2–3 minutes or until lightly golden brown, stirring continuously.

Arrange the shredded chicken and remaining cilantro leaves over the bean salad and sprinkle with the toasted coconut and alfalfa shoots, if using. Serve with the remaining dressing.

For shrimp, avocado, & coconut salad, make as above, replacing the chicken with 8 oz cooked, peeled shrimps. Dice the flesh of 1 firm, ripe avocado, toss in 1 tablespoon of lime juice, and add to the bean salad. Serve as above.

thai red chicken curry

Serves **4**
Preparation time **15 minutes**
Cooking time **35 minutes**

1 tablespoon **sunflower oil**
3 **shallots**, finely chopped
3 **garlic cloves**, finely chopped
2 tablespoons **Thai red curry paste**
2 teaspoons **galangal paste**
1¾ cups **reduced-fat coconut milk**
2 teaspoons **Thai fish sauce**
1 teaspoon **palm sugar** or **light brown sugar**
3 **kaffir lime leaves**
6 boneless, skinless **chicken thighs**, diced
handful of **Thai basil leaves** (optional)

Heat the oil in a saucepan over a medium heat, add the shallots and garlic and fry for 3–4 minutes until softened. Stir in the curry paste and galangal paste and cook for 1 minute. Mix in the coconut milk, fish sauce, sugar, and lime leaves and bring to a boil.

Stir in the chicken, then reduce the heat, cover, and simmer for 30 minutes, or until the chicken is cooked through, stirring occasionally. Stir in the basil leaves, if using, and serve with boiled rice.

For Thai green chicken curry, make the curry as above, adding 2 peeled and finely chopped lemon grass stalks when frying the shallots and garlic. Replace the red curry paste with 2 tablespoons Thai green curry paste and stir in, then continue as above. To finish, stir in the grated zest of 1 lime and lime juice to taste, garnish with chopped cilantro, and serve immediately.

lemony poached chicken

Serves **4**
Preparation time **10 minutes**
Cooking time **1¾–2 hours**

1 whole **free-range chicken**,
  about 3–4 lb
3 **shallots**, halved
2 **garlic cloves**, lightly crushed
1 **celery stick**, roughly
  chopped
1 **rosemary sprig**
8 **black peppercorns**
6 tablespoons **balsamic
  vinegar**
1 **preserved lemon**, chopped
1 small bunch of **sage**, leaves
  removed
2 tablespoons **extra virgin
  canola oil**
salt and **pepper**

Place the chicken, shallots, garlic, celery, rosemary, and black peppercorns in a large saucepan. Add the balsamic vinegar and pour in enough cold water to almost cover the chicken. Place over a medium heat and bring slowly to a boil, skimming the surface to remove any scummy froth. Cover and simmer gently for 1 hour.

Add the preserved lemon and half the sage leaves, then simmer gently for an additional 15–30 minutes, depending on the size of the chicken, until the juices run clear when the thickest part of the leg is pierced with a knife. Carefully remove from the pan and place in a deep dish, cover with foil, and allow to rest. Increase the heat and boil the stock for 20–25 minutes or until reduced by half. Remove from the heat and allow to cool slightly. Season to taste.

Heat the oil in a small skillet and pan-fry the remaining sage leaves for 30 seconds until crisp. Remove with a slotted spoon and drain on paper towels.

Cut the chicken meat from the carcass, discarding the skin, and spoon into shallow bowls with plenty of cooking broth. Garnish with the crisp sage leaves and serve with steamed asparagus and broccoli.

For lemony chicken breasts, replace the whole chicken with 4 large boneless, skinless chicken breasts. Place in a large saucepan with the garlic, rosemary, peppercorns, balsamic vinegar, and preserved lemon and just cover with water. Simmer gently for about 12 minutes or until the chicken is cooked through. Cut the chicken into thick slices and serve in bowls with the chicken broth, garnished with sage leaves as above.

chicken & pickled walnut pilaf

Serves **4**
Preparation time **20 minutes**
Cooking time **about
  35 minutes**

13 oz boneless, skinless
  chicken thighs, diced
2 teaspoons **Moroccan
  spice blend** (see below for
  homemade)
4 tablespoons **olive oil**
⅓ cup **pine nuts**
1 large **onion**, chopped
3 **garlic cloves**, sliced
½ teaspoon **ground turmeric**
1¼ cups **mixed long-grain
  and wild rice**
1¼ cups **chicken stock**
3 pieces of **stem ginger**, finely
  chopped
3 tablespoons chopped
  parsley
2 tablespoons chopped **mint**
2 oz **pickled walnuts**, sliced
salt and **pepper**

Mix the chicken with the spice blend and a little salt in a bowl.

Heat the oil in a large skillet over a medium heat, add the pine nuts and fry until beginning to brown. Remove with a slotted spoon and drain on paper towels. Add the chicken to the pan and fry gently for 6–8 minutes, or until lightly browned, stirring occasionally.

Stir in the onion and fry for 5 minutes. Add the garlic and turmeric and fry for another 1 minute. Add the rice and stock and bring to a boil, then reduce the heat to low and simmer very gently for about 15 minutes or until the chicken is cooked through, the rice is tender, and the stock absorbed. Add a little water if the liquid has been absorbed before the rice is cooked through.

Stir in the ginger, parsley, mint, walnuts, and pine nuts. Season with salt and pepper to taste and heat through gently for 2 minutes before serving.

For homemade Moroccan spice blend, mix together ½ teaspoon each of crushed fennel, cumin, coriander, and mustard seeds with ¼ teaspoon each of ground cloves and cinnamon.

asian ground turkey salad

Serves **4**
Preparation time **20 minutes**
Cooking time **8–10 minutes**

1 lb **ground turkey**
2 **garlic cloves**, finely chopped
1 **shallot**, finely chopped
1 small **red chili**, seeded and
   finely chopped
1½ tablespoons **peanut oil**
½ **Chinese cabbage**,
   shredded
1½ cups **snow peas**,
   shredded
½ small **cucumber**, cut into
   thin matchsticks
2½ cups **bean sprouts**
1 **carrot**, peeled and cut into
   thin matchsticks
3 **scallions**, thinly sliced
4 tablespoons **unsalted
   peanuts**, chopped
chopped **cilantro**

Dressing
1½ teaspoons peeled and
   grated **fresh ginger root**
1½ teaspoons **fish sauce**
1 tablespoon **light soy sauce**
2 tablespoons **lime juice**
2 tablespoons **peanut oil**
1½ teaspoons **palm sugar**

Mix together the turkey, garlic, shallot, and chili in a bowl. Heat the oil in a large skillet over a medium-high heat, add the turkey mixture and then stir-fry for 8–10 minutes or until the meat is browned and cooked through. Tip into a large bowl.

Beat together all the dressing ingredients in a small bowl and pour over the cooked turkey. Allow to cool for 10 minutes.

Meanwhile, mix together the Chinese cabbage, snow peas, cucumber, bean sprouts, carrot, and scallions in a bowl. Pile onto serving plates and spoon over the turkey. Sprinkle with the peanuts and cilantro and serve immediately with lime wedges on the side.

For Asian-style pork wraps, replace the turkey with 1 lb ground pork. Prepare as above, keeping the Chinese cabbage whole and separate from the salad. Serve the whole leaves, dressed pork, and salad in 3 separate piles. To eat, pile the mixed salad and ground pork into the whole leaves, sprinkle with the cilantro and peanuts, and fold to create a wrap before eating.

duck, pear, & pomegranate salad

Serves **4**
Preparation time **15 minutes**
Cooking time **15–20 minutes**

2 large, lean **duck breasts**
2 **Comice pears**, cored and
diced
2½ cups **mixed leaf and herb
salad**
⅓ cup **walnut pieces**
1 **pomegranate**, seeds
removed

Dressing
2 teaspoons **lime juice**
2 teaspoons **raspberry
vinegar**
2 teaspoons **pomegranate
molasses** (optional—see
right for homemade)
2 tablespoons **walnut oil**
salt and **pepper**

Remove any excess fat from the duck breasts and score the surface using a sharp knife. Heat a ridged griddle pan until hot, then add the duck breasts, skin side down, and cook for 8–10 minutes. Turn them over and cook for an additional 5–10 minutes or until cooked to the pinkness desired. Remove from the pan, cover with foil, and allow to rest.

Mix together the pears and leaf salad in a bowl. Arrange on serving plates and sprinkle with the walnut pieces.

Beat together all the dressing ingredients in a bowl and season to taste. Drizzle over the salad.

Slice the duck breasts and arrange on the salad. Sprinkle with the pomegranate seeds and serve immediately.

For homemade pomegranate molasses, juice 2 large pomegranates with a citrus press or remove the seeds and pulse in a food processor or blender. Pour the juice into a small saucepan, add 1 tablespoon sugar, and stir until the sugar dissolves. Bring to a boil, then reduce the heat and simmer rapidly until reduced to a thick, sticky molasses. Cool and store in an airtight bottle in the refrigerator for up to 2 weeks.

vegetarian

lemony mushroom spaghetti

Serves **4**
Preparation time **8 minutes**
Cooking time **18–20 minutes**

8 oz **chestnut mushrooms**
1 **garlic clove**, finely chopped
2 tablespoons **olive oil**
13 oz **whole-wheat spaghetti**
3 cups fresh **whole-wheat bread crumbs**
finely grated zest and juice of 1 **lemon**
1 small bunch of **parsley**, chopped
½ teaspoon **red pepper flakes** (optional)
salt and **pepper**
grated **Parmesan cheese**, to serve (optional)

Place the mushrooms, stalk side up, in a large roasting pan. Sprinkle with the garlic, drizzle with the oil, and season generously with salt and pepper. Place in a preheated oven, 350°F, for 18–20 minutes or until tender and juicy.

Meanwhile, cook the pasta in a large saucepan of boiling water for 10–12 minutes, or according to the package instructions, until al dente.

Put the bread crumbs, lemon zest, half of the parsley, and the red pepper flakes, if using, into a large, nonstick skillet over a medium-high heat. Dry-fry for 4–5 minutes, or until golden brown and crispy, stirring continuously. Set aside.

Remove the mushrooms from the oven and cool slightly, then roughly chop. Drain the pasta and toss with the mushrooms, lemon juice, and remaining parsley. Season with salt and pepper to taste, then heap into serving bowls. Sprinkle with the bread crumbs and serve immediately with Parmesan, if desired.

For wild mushroom pasta, cook the spaghetti as above. Roughly chop 5 oz chestnut mushrooms. Heat the oil in a large skillet over a medium-high heat, then add the mushrooms and garlic and fry for 3–4 minutes until softened. Roughly chop a drained 9 oz jar mixed or wild mushrooms, add to the pan and heat through. Stir in the lemon juice and zest, chopped parsley, and red pepper flakes, if using. Toss with the drained pasta, season to taste, and serve.

penne with peas & beans

Serves **4**
Preparation time **5 minutes**
Cooking time **10–12 minutes**

13 oz **whole-wheat penne**
1 tablespoon **extra virgin
    canola oil** or **olive oil**
2 **scallions**, finely chopped
1 cup **reduced-fat
    mascarpone cheese**
4 tablespoons **lemon juice**
1²/₃ cups **frozen peas**, thawed
1½ cups **frozen baby fava
    beans**, thawed
1 small bunch of **basil**, roughly
    chopped, a few leaves
    reserved for garnish
salt and **pepper**

Cook the penne in a large saucepan of boiling water for 10–12 minutes, or according to the package instructions, until al dente.

Meanwhile, heat the oil in a large skillet over a medium-low heat, add the scallions and fry for 1–2 minutes or until softened. Stir in the mascarpone, lemon juice, peas, fava beans, and basil. Season with salt and pepper to taste and stir for 1–2 minutes or until bubbling.

Drain the penne, reserving 3 tablespoons of the cooking water. Stir the pasta and the reserved liquid into the creamy peas and beans. Serve immediately, garnished with extra basil leaves.

For fava bean & pea risotto, melt 2 tablespoons butter with 1 tablespoon olive oil and cook the scallions until softened. Add 1¾ cups risotto rice and stir for 1–2 minutes or until translucent. Add ¾ cup white wine, then 4 cups boiling vegetable stock, a small ladleful at a time and stirring constantly, only adding more once the rice has absorbed the previous ladleful. Continue until all the liquid has been absorbed and the rice is just cooked. This should take about 18 minutes. Stir in the peas, beans, and basil 2 minutes before the end of the cooking time. Remove from the heat, stir in ½ cup mascarpone and serve immediately.

spicy lentils & chickpeas

Serves **4**
Preparation time **15 minutes**
Cooking time **about**
  35 minutes

1 tablespoon **peanut oil**
1 **onion**, finely chopped
2 **garlic cloves**, thinly sliced
2 **celery sticks**, diced
1 **green bell pepper**, cored,
  seeded, and chopped
¾ cup **red lentils**, rinsed
2 teaspoons **garam masala**
1 teaspoon **cumin seeds**
½ teaspoon **hot chili powder**
1 teaspoon **ground coriander**
2 tablespoons **tomato paste**
3 cups hot **vegetable stock**
13 oz can **chickpeas**, drained
salt and **pepper**
2 tablespoons chopped
  cilantro, to garnish

Heat the oil in a heavy saucepan over a medium heat, add the onion, garlic, celery, and green pepper and fry gently for 10–12 minutes or until softened and beginning to brown.

Stir in the lentils and spices and cook for 2–3 minutes, stirring frequently. Add the tomato paste, stock, and chickpeas and bring to a boil. Reduce the heat, cover, and simmer gently for about 20 minutes or until the lentils collapse. Season with salt and pepper to taste.

Ladle into bowls and sprinkle with the cilantro. Serve immediately with boiled brown rice and cooling, spiced yogurt (see below).

For cooling, spiced yogurt, to serve as an accompaniment, mix together ¾ cup fat-free plain yogurt, 2 tablespoons lemon juice, and ½ teaspoon of garam masala in a small bowl. Fold in ½ small, seeded and grated cucumber, then season with salt and pepper to taste. Serve sprinkled with 1 tablespoon chopped cilantro.

veggie stir-fry with bok choy

Serves **4**
Preparation time **10 minutes**
Cooking time **5–7 minutes**

8 small **bok choy**, about
   1 ¼ lb in total
1 tablespoon **peanut oil**
2 **garlic cloves**, thinly sliced
1 inch piece of **fresh ginger
   root**, peeled and finely
   chopped
7 oz **sugar snap peas**, sliced
   diagonally
7 oz **asparagus tips**, sliced in
   half lengthwise
7 oz **baby corn**, sliced in half
   lengthwise
⅔ cup podded **edamame
   beans** or 2 cups **bean
   sprouts**
⅔ cup **sweet teriyaki sauce**

Cut the bok choy in half, or into thick slices if large, and put in a steamer basket. Lower into a shallow saucepan of boiling water so that the bok choy is not quite touching the water. Cover and steam for 2–3 minutes or until tender. Alternatively, use a bamboo or electric steamer.

Heat a large wok or skillet over a high heat until smoking hot, add the oil, garlic, and ginger and stir-fry for 30 seconds. Add the vegetables and stir continuously for 2–3 minutes or until beginning to wilt.

Pour over the sweet teriyaki sauce, toss to combine, and serve immediately with the steamed bok choy and steamed rice, if desired.

For sweet chili vegetable stir-fry, heat the oil in the wok and stir-fry 1 thinly sliced onion with the garlic and ginger. Add 1 carrot, cut into thin matchsticks, and 2 cups sliced mushrooms and stir-fry for 2 minutes. Stir in 2 cups bean sprouts and 6 cups shredded spinach for another minute until wilted. Stir in ¾ cup sweet chili stir-fry sauce and serve immediately with the bok choy or cooked noodles.

roasted peppers with quinoa

Serves **4**
Preparation time **15 minutes**
Cooking time **45 minutes**

2 romano or **long red sweet
peppers**, halved, cored, and
seeded
2 large **yellow bell peppers**,
halved, cored, and seeded
20 **red** and **yellow cherry
tomatoes**, halved
1 teaspoon **cumin seeds**
2 tablespoons **olive oil**
1 ¼ cups **quinoa**
1 **onion**, finely chopped
½ teaspoon **ground ginger**
1 teaspoon **paprika**
pinch of **nutmeg**
⅓ cup ready-to-eat **dried
apricots**, chopped
⅓ cup **raisins**
⅓ cup pitted chopped **dates**
½ cup shelled **pistachio nuts**
¼ cup **slivered almonds**,
toasted, plus extra to garnish
2 **scallions**, finely sliced
salt and **pepper**

Fill the red peppers with the yellow cherry tomatoes and the yellow peppers with the red tomatoes. Sprinkle with the cumin seeds, drizzle with 1 tablespoon of the oil, and season well with salt and pepper. Place in a preheated oven, 350°F, for about 45 minutes or until tender and slightly blackened around the edges.

Meanwhile, rinse the quinoa several times in cold water. Pour into a pan with twice its volume of boiling water, cover and simmer for about 12 minutes. It is cooked when the seed is coming away from the germ. Remove from the heat, cover, and allow to stand until all the water has been absorbed.

Heat the remaining oil in a small skillet over a medium heat, add the onion and cook for 10 minutes or until softened. Add the spices, dried fruits, and nuts and cook for an additional 3–4 minutes, or until the fruits have softened, stirring frequently. Gently fold into the cooked quinoa.

Heap the quinoa onto 4 plates and top each with 1 red and 1 yellow pepper half. Sprinkle with the scallions and extra slivered almonds and serve.

For quinoa-stuffed peppers, make the fruit and nut quinoa as above. Cut 10 cherry tomatoes into quarters and mix with the quinoa. Spoon into the halved peppers and top with 5 oz sliced reduced-fat feta or goat cheese. Drizzle with a little olive oil, the cumin seeds, and season with salt and pepper. Place in the oven for 45 minutes or until the peppers are tender. Serve as above with salad leaves.

veggie kebabs with bulghur wheat

Serves **4**

Preparation time **20 minutes**

Cooking time **20–25 minutes**

1 small **red bell pepper**, cored
and seeded

1 small **yellow bell pepper**,
cored and seeded

2 small **zucchini**, thickly sliced

1 small **eggplant**, cut into
chunks

1 small **red onion**, quartered

8 **chestnut mushrooms**,
halved

2 teaspoons **dried rosemary**

2 tablespoons **olive oil**

grated zest of 1 **lemon**

1 teaspoon **fennel seeds**

salt and **pepper**

Bulghur wheat salad

3 cups **vegetable stock**

1 ¼ cups **coarse bulghur
wheat**

1 tablespoon **harissa**

½ cup **raisins**

2 **scallions**, finely sliced

2 tablespoons chopped **mint**

½ cup **sunflower seeds**

Cut the red and yellow peppers into large pieces and place in a bowl with the other vegetables. Toss with the dried rosemary, oil, lemon zest, and fennel seeds and season with salt and pepper. Thread onto 4 long or 8 short metal skewers and cook under a medium-hot broiler for 20–25 minutes, or until tender and browned, turning occasionally.

Meanwhile, put the stock in a saucepan and bring to a boil. Add the bulghur wheat, cover, and simmer for 7 minutes. Remove from the heat and allow to stand until the liquid has been absorbed. Fork the harissa, raisins, scallions, mint, and sunflower seeds through the cooked bulghur wheat until well combined, then spoon onto serving plates.

Arrange the vegetable kebabs on the plates with the bulghur wheat salad and serve immediately.

For minted yogurt, to serve as an accompaniment, mix together 1 cup fat-free plain yogurt, ½ teaspoon fennel seeds, 2 tablespoons lemon juice, and 3 tablespoons chopped mint in a serving dish and season to taste.

squash, carrot, & mango tagine

Serves **4**
Preparation time **15 minutes**
Cooking time **35–40 minutes**

2 tablespoons **olive oil**
1 large **onion**, cut into large
   chunks
3 **garlic cloves**, finely chopped
1 **butternut squash**, about
   1¾ lb in total, peeled,
   seeded, and cubed
2 small **carrots**, peeled and
   cut into thick batons
½ x 1 inch **cinnamon stick**
½ teaspoon **turmeric**
¼ teaspoon **cayenne pepper**
   (optional)
½ teaspoon ground **cumin**
1 teaspoon **paprika**
pinch of **saffron threads**
1 tablespoon **tomato paste**
3 cups hot **vegetable stock**
1 **mango**, peeled, pitted, and
   cut into 1 inch chunks
salt and **pepper**
2 tablespoons chopped
   cilantro, to garnish

Heat the oil in a large, heavy saucepan over a medium heat, add the onion and cook for 5 minutes or until beginning to soften. Add the garlic, squash, carrots, and spices and fry gently for another 5 minutes.

Stir in the tomato paste, then pour in the stock and season with salt and pepper to taste. Cover and simmer gently for 20–25 minutes or until the vegetables are tender. Stir in the mango and simmer gently for an additional 5 minutes.

Ladle the tagine into serving bowls and sprinkle with the cilantro and serve with steamed couscous.

For spicy squash & carrot soup, make the tagine as above, adding an extra 1 cup vegetable stock. Once the vegetables are tender, place in a food processor or blender and blend until smooth. Ladle into bowls and serve sprinkled with the chopped cilantro.

roasted beet & bean salad

Serves **4**
Preparation time **10 minutes**
Cooking time **about 1 hour
10 minutes**

2 lb raw **beets**, peeled
1½ tablespoons **extra virgin
canola oil**, plus extra to
serve
2 teaspoons **cumin seeds**
4 tablespoons **balsamic
vinegar**
2 cups **green beans**, trimmed
1 **red onion**, thinly sliced
1 cup **ricotta cheese**
finely grated zest of 1 **lemon**
1 small bunch of **basil**,
chopped, a few leaves
reserved for garnish
1 **multigrain** or **cereal
baguette**, sliced
1 tablespoon **balsamic glaze**
salt and **pepper**

Cut the beets into wedges or in half, if small. Toss with the oil and cumin seeds and season with salt and pepper. Tip into a roasting pan and place in a preheated oven, 350°F, for 45 minutes. Pour over the balsamic vinegar and toss to coat. Return to the oven for an additional 20 minutes or until the beetroot is tender and slightly sticky.

Cook the beans in a large saucepan of lightly salted boiling water for 2–3 minutes or until just tender. Drain and toss with the beets and onion in a bowl.

Mix together in a bowl the ricotta, lemon zest, and basil and season with salt and pepper. Spread over the baguette slices, place on a broiler pan and cook under a preheated medium-hot broiler for 3 minutes or until hot and lightly golden.

Heap the beet and bean salad into bowls and top with the ricotta croutons. Drizzle with a little balsamic glaze and extra virgin canola oil and sprinkle with the extra basil leaves. Serve immediately.

For wintery roasted parsnip & carrot salad, mix together 1 lb parsnips and 1 lb carrots, both cut into batons, the oil, cumin seeds, and 3–4 thyme sprigs in a roasting pan. Place in the preheated oven for about 30 minutes or until tender. Spoon into a serving dish and drizzle over 2 tablespoons honey mixed with 1 tablespoon balsamic vinegar. Make the croutons as above, replacing the basil with 1 bunch of thyme. Serve the roasted vegetables with salad leaves, sprinkled with 2 tablespoons toasted hazelnuts, if desired.

chickpea & feta salad

Serves **4**
Preparation time **10 minutes**
Cooking time **5–7 minutes**

13 oz can **chickpeas**, drained
1 **Lebanese cucumber** or
 ½ **cucumber**, diced
5 oz **radishes**, thinly sliced
1 cup **red seedless grapes**,
 halved
1 small **radicchio**, sliced
7 oz **reduced-fat feta cheese**,
 cut into 4 pieces
2 tablespoons **extra virgin
 canola** or **olive oil**
½ teaspoon **dried oregano**
2 heaping tablespoons
 pumpkin seeds
small handful of **radish
 sprouts** (optional)
salt and **pepper**
lemon wedges, to serve

Mix together the chickpeas, cucumber, radishes, and grapes in a large bowl. Toss lightly with the radicchio, season with salt and pepper, and pile into serving dishes.

Place the feta on a foil-lined broiler pan, drizzle with 2 teaspoons of the oil, and sprinkle with the dried oregano and a little pepper. Cook under a preheated broiler for 3–4 minutes or until golden. Remove from the broiler and allow to cool for 2–3 minutes.

Heat a small nonstick skillet over a medium heat, add the pumpkin seeds and dry-fry for 2–3 minutes or until lightly golden. Tip onto a small plate.

Arrange the broiled feta on the salad. Sprinkle with the toasted pumpkin seeds and radish sprouts, if using. Drizzle with the remaining oil and serve immediately with the lemon wedges.

For watermelon & haloumi salad, mix together ½ peeled watermelon, cut into large chunks, with 2 tablespoons chopped mint, ½ finely chopped red onion, 16–20 pitted black olives, and the chickpeas. Replace the feta with 7 oz haloumi cheese and cut into slices. Brush with the oil and broil as above. Serve with the pumpkin seeds as above.

baked mushroom risotto

Serves **4**
Preparation time **15 minutes**
Cooking time 1¼ **hours**

1 cup **dried porcini mushrooms**, soaked in ½ cup boiling water for 10–15 minutes
2 tablespoons **butter**
1 tablespoon **olive oil**
2 **shallots**, finely chopped
1 **leek**, trimmed, cleaned, and finely chopped
1 large **garlic clove**, finely chopped
1¾ cups **short-grain brown rice**
3 tablespoons **Marsala**
5 cups **vegetable stock**
4 oz **asparagus tips**, chopped
salt and **pepper**
finely grated **Parmesan cheese**, to serve (optional)

Drain the porcini, reserving the soaking liquid, then squeeze dry and roughly chop.

Heat the butter and oil in a large, flameproof casserole over a low heat, add the shallots and leek and fry gently for 8 minutes or until softened. Add the garlic and fry for an additional 2 minutes. Stir the rice into the pan and cook for 1–2 minutes, then pour over the Marsala and bubble, stirring continuously, until evaporated.

Mix in the mushrooms, reserved soaking liquid, and stock, stir well and bring to a boil. Season to taste with salt and pepper, cover, and place in a preheated oven, 350°F, for 45 minutes, stirring occasionally.

Add the asparagus and stir well. Return to the oven for another 15 minutes or until the rice is tender and most of the liquid has been absorbed. Remove from the oven and allow to stand for 2–3 minutes. Spoon the risotto into serving bowls and sprinkle with the grated Parmesan, if desired.

For Asian-style baked risotto, make as above, replacing the porcini mushrooms with 1 cup dried shiitake mushrooms, the Marsala with 3 tablespoons sake, the vegetable stock with 5 cups instant miso soup, and the asparagus tips with 2 small, sliced bok choy.

artichoke & asparagus pizzas

Serves **4**
Preparation time **20 minutes**, plus rising
Cooking time **45 minutes**

3¼ cups **whole-wheat flour**
1 x ¼ oz **envelope instant dry yeast**
2 teaspoons **sugar,** plus a pinch
1½ teaspoons **salt**
2 tablespoons **olive oil**
1 cup hand-hot **water**
2 **garlic cloves**, finely chopped
1¼ cups **basil** and **onion-flavored pureed tomatoes**
1½ teaspoons **dried oregano**
13 oz can **artichokes** in water, drained and thickly sliced
7 oz **asparagus tips**
1 cup **ricotta cheese**
1 cup finely grated **reduced-fat sharp cheddar cheese** (optional)
handful of **arugula leaves**
chili oil, for drizzling (optional)
salt and **pepper**

Put the flour, yeast, 2 teaspoons sugar, and the salt in a bowl. Pour in 1 tablespoon of the oil and measurement water and mix to a dough. Turn the dough out onto a lightly floured surface and knead for 4–5 minutes until smooth and elastic. Place in a lightly oiled bowl, cover with oiled plastic wrap, and leave in a warm place to rise for 1½ hours or until doubled in size.

Meanwhile, heat the remaining oil in a saucepan over a low heat, add the garlic and cook for 1 minute. Stir in the tomatoes, ½ teaspoon of the oregano, and a pinch of sugar and season with salt and pepper to taste. Simmer for 30 minutes or until thick. Heat a griddle pan, add the artichokes and cook for 3–4 minutes, turning once, or until slightly charred. Repeat with the asparagus.

Divide the dough into 4 and roll out on a floured surface until about 8 inches in diameter. Place the bases on lightly greased baking sheets, cover, and allow to rise for an additional 30–45 minutes. Thinly spread the sauce over the bases and arrange the griddled vegetables on top. Add teaspoons of ricotta and the cheddar, if using. Sprinkle with the remaining oregano.

Place in a preheated oven, 400°F, for 12–15 minutes or until bubbling and the bases are crisp. Serve topped with the arugula and drizzled with a little chili oil, if desired.

For quick pita pizzas, spread a little basil and garlic-flavored pureed tomatoes over 4 whole-wheat pita breads. Top with 7 oz char-grilled vegetables and the ricotta, cheddar, and oregano, as above. Place under a preheated broiler for 4–5 minutes or until bubbling.

warm lentil, tomato, & onion salad

Serves **4**
Preparation time **10 minutes**
Cooking time **40–45 minutes**

1 tablespoon **olive oil**
1 large **red onion**, thinly sliced
2 oz **fresh ginger root**, peeled
and chopped
4 **garlic cloves**, thinly sliced
½ cup **green lentils**, rinsed
½ cup **red lentils**, rinsed
½ teaspoon **ground
cinnamon**
13 oz **tomatoes**, roughly
chopped, or 13 oz can
chopped tomatoes
1½ cups **water** or **vegetable
stock**
2 teaspoons **black onion
seeds**
salt and **pepper**
parsley, to garnish
lemon wedges, to serve

Heat the oil in a large, heavy saucepan over a medium-low heat, add the onion, ginger, and garlic and cook gently for 10 minutes until softened but not browned.

Stir the lentils and cinnamon into the onions. Add the tomatoes and measurement water or stock. Season with salt and pepper and bring to a boil. Reduce the heat, cover, and allow to simmer gently for 30–35 minutes or until the lentils are tender and the liquid has been absorbed.

Spoon the lentils into bowls and sprinkle with the black onion seeds and garnish with parsley leaves. Serve warm with lemon wedges and toasted whole-wheat flatbreads, if desired.

For no-cook lentil, tomato, & onion salad, rinse and drain an 8 oz package cooked lentils. Place in a bowl and mix with ½ finely chopped red onion, 4 chopped tomatoes, a small crushed garlic clove, a ½ inch piece of peeled and finely grated fresh ginger root and 2 tablespoons chopped parsley. Make a dressing with 1 tablespoon olive oil, 2 tablespoons lemon juice, pinch of ground cinnamon, pinch of ground paprika, and some salt and pepper. Toss the lentil salad in the dressing and serve, garnished, as above.

bean chili with avocado salsa

Serves **4–6**
Preparation time **15 minutes**
Cooking time **30 minutes**

3 tablespoons **olive oil**
2 teaspoons **cumin seeds**, crushed
1 teaspoon **dried oregano**
1 **red onion**, chopped
1 **celery stick**, chopped
1 **red chili**, seeded and sliced
2 x 13 oz cans **chopped tomatoes**
1 cup **sundried tomatoes**, thinly sliced
2 teaspoons **sugar**
1 ¼ cups **vegetable stock**
2 x 13 oz cans **red kidney beans**, drained
handful of **cilantro**, chopped
6 tablespoons **low-fat sour cream**
salt and **pepper**

Salsa
1 small **avocado**
2 **tomatoes**
2 tablespoons **sweet chili sauce**
2 teaspoons **lime juice**

Heat the oil in a large saucepan over a medium-low heat, add the cumin seeds, oregano, onion, celery, and chili and cook gently, stirring frequently, for about 6–8 minutes or until the vegetables are beginning to brown.

Add the canned tomatoes, sundried tomatoes, sugar, stock, beans, and cilantro and bring to a boil. Reduce the heat and simmer for about 20 minutes or until the juices are thickened and pulpy.

Make the salsa. Peel, pit, and finely dice the avocado and put it in a small bowl. Halve the tomatoes, scoop out the seeds and finely dice the flesh. Add to the bowl along with the chili sauce and lime juice. Mix well.

Season the bean mixture with salt and pepper and spoon into bowls. Top with spoonfuls of sour cream and the avocado salsa. Serve with toasted pita or flatbreads.

For bean stew, heat 4 tablespoons olive oil in a small saucepan, add 2 crushed garlic cloves, 1 tablespoon chopped rosemary, and 2 teaspoons grated lemon zest and gently fry for 3 minutes. Add 2 x 13 oz cans lima beans with their liquid, 4 large skinned and chopped tomatoes, and a little chili powder. Bring to a boil, then simmer over a high heat for 8–10 minutes or until the sauce is thickened. Season and serve with the avocado salsa and sour cream.

gingered tofu & mango salad

Serves **2**
Preparation time **15 minutes**,
  plus marinating
Cooking time **5 minutes**

1 oz **fresh ginger root**, peeled
  and grated
2 tablespoons **light soy sauce**
1 **garlic clove**, finely chopped
1 tablespoon **seasoned rice
  vinegar**
4 oz **firm silken tofu**, cut into
  ½ inch cubes
2 tablespoons **peanut** or
  vegetable oil
1 bunch of **scallions**, sliced
  diagonally into ¾ inch
  lengths
⅓ cup **cashew nuts**
1 small **mango**, peeled, pitted,
  and sliced
½ small **iceberg lettuce**,
  shredded

Mix together the ginger, soy sauce, garlic, and vinegar in a small bowl. Add the tofu to the bowl and toss the ingredients together. Allow to marinate for 15 minutes.

Lift the tofu from the marinade with a fork, drain it, and reserve the marinade. Heat the oil in a skillet over a medium heat, add the tofu pieces and gently fry for 3 minutes or until golden. Remove with a slotted spoon and keep warm.

Add the scallions and cashews to the pan and fry quickly for 30 seconds. Add the mango slices to the pan and cook for 30 seconds or until heated through.

Pile the lettuce onto serving plates and arrange the tofu, scallions, mango, and cashews over the top. Heat the marinade juices in the pan with 2 tablespoons water, pour the mixture over the salad, and serve immediately.

For tofu & sugar snap salad, marinate and fry the tofu as above. Add the scallions and cashews to the pan, also adding 1 red chili, sliced into rounds, and 4 oz halved sugar snap peas. Omit the mango. Fry for 1 minute until heated through, then gently toss in the fried tofu. Add the juice of ½ lime and 2 tablespoons water to the reserved marinade and drizzle it over the salad before serving on the lettuce.

pumpkin & root vegetable stew

Serves **8–10**
Preparation time **20 minutes**
Cooking time **1½–2 hours**

1 **pumpkin**, about 3 lb
4 tablespoons **sunflower** or
   olive oil
1 large **onion**, finely chopped
3–4 **garlic cloves**, finely
   chopped
1 small **red chili**, seeded and
   chopped
4 **celery sticks**, cut into
   1 inch lengths
1 lb **carrots**, cut into 1 inch
   pieces
8 oz **parsnips**, cut into 1 inch
   pieces
2 x 13 oz cans **plum
   tomatoes**
3 tablespoons **tomato paste**
1–2 tablespoons **hot paprika**
1 cup **vegetable stock**
1 **bouquet garni**
2 x 13 oz cans **red kidney
   beans**, drained
salt and **pepper**
3–4 tablespoons finely
   chopped **parsley**, to garnish

Slice the pumpkin in half and discard the seeds and fibers. Cut the flesh into cubes, removing the skin. You should have about 2 lb pumpkin flesh.

Heat the oil in a large saucepan over a medium heat, add the onion, garlic, and chili and fry until softened but not browned. Add the pumpkin and celery and fry gently for 10 minutes.

Stir in the carrots, parsnips, tomatoes, tomato paste, paprika, stock, and bouquet garni. Bring to a boil, then reduce the heat, cover the pan, and simmer for 1–1½ hours or until the vegetables are almost tender.

Add the beans and cook for 10 minutes. Season with salt and pepper and sprinkle with the parsley. Serve with crusty bread or garlic mashed potatoes. This stew improves with reheating.

For pumpkin goulash, heat 2 tablespoons oil in a large, heavy saucepan and fry 1 chopped onion until softened. Stir in 1 tablespoon paprika and 1 teaspoon caraway seeds and cook for 1 minute. Add a 13 oz can chopped tomatoes and 2 tablespoons dark brown sugar and bring to a boil. Add 3 cups thickly sliced pumpkin, 2 cups diced potatoes, a large sliced carrot, and 1 seeded and chopped red bell pepper. Season, cover, and bring to a boil, then simmer for 1–1½ hours. To serve, stir in ⅔ cup low-fat sour cream.

saffron-scented vegetable tagine

Serves **4**
Preparation time **15 minutes**
Cooking time **50 minutes**

6 tablespoons **sunflower oil**
1 large **onion**, finely chopped
2 **garlic cloves**, finely chopped
2 teaspoons **ground coriander**
2 teaspoons **ground cumin**
2 teaspoons **ground cinnamon**
13 oz can **chickpeas**, drained
13 oz can **chopped tomatoes**
2½ cups **vegetable stock**
¼ teaspoon **saffron threads**
1 large **eggplant**, chopped
8 oz **button mushrooms**, halved if large
⅔ cup chopped **dried figs**
2 tablespoons chopped **cilantro**
salt and **pepper**

Heat 2 tablespoons of the oil in a skillet over a medium heat, add the onion, garlic, and spices and cook, stirring frequently, for 5 minutes or until golden. Using a slotted spoon, transfer to a saucepan and add the chickpeas, tomatoes, stock, and saffron. Season with salt and pepper.

Heat the remaining oil in the skillet over a high heat, add the eggplant and cook, stirring frequently, for 5 minutes or until browned. Add to the stew and bring to a boil, then reduce the heat, cover, and simmer gently for 20 minutes.

Stir in the mushrooms and figs and simmer gently, uncovered, for an additional 20 minutes. Stir in the chopped cilantro and season to taste. Serve with steamed whole-wheat couscous.

For winter vegetable & lentil tagine, replace the eggplant with 2 sliced carrots and 2 cubed potatoes. Instead of the chickpeas use a drained 13 oz can green lentils. Make as above, replacing the figs with ⅔ cup ready-to-eat dried apricots.

and to
finish....

elderflower poached pears

Serves **4**

Preparation time **5 minutes**,
  plus cooling

Cooking time **about
  25 minutes**

½ cup **elderflower and pear
  or elderflower and apple
  cordial**

2 cups **apple juice**

2 teaspoons **lemon juice**

4 large **pears**, peeled, cored,
  and quartered

pinch of **saffron threads**

Mix the cordial, apple juice, and lemon juice in a small,
deep saucepan. Bring to a gentle simmer and add the
pears and saffron. Simmer gently for about 25 minutes
or until the pears are tender.

Remove from the heat, cover, and allow to cool
completely in the poaching liquid. Carefully remove
the pears with a slotted spoon and divide into serving
bowls. Ladle over the poaching liquid to serve.

For baked apples in elderflower & saffron, replace
the pears with 4 peeled, cored, and quartered apples
and place in a deep ovenproof dish. Heat the cordial,
apple juice, and saffron as above, omitting the lemon
juice, and pour over the apples. Cover with foil and
place in a preheated oven, 350 °F, for about 1 hour or
until the apples are tender.

autumn fruit oaty crumble

Serves **4**
Preparation time **15 minutes**
Cooking time **40–45 minutes**

1 **dessert apple**, peeled,
  cored, and sliced
1/3 cup chopped ready-to-eat
  dried apples (optional)
13 oz can **pear halves** in juice,
  drained with 4 tablespoons
  juice reserved, roughly
  chopped
7 oz ripe **plums**, halved, pitted,
  and quartered
3 tablespoons **raisins** or
  golden raisins

Topping
3/4 cup **whole-wheat flour**
1/2 cup **rolled oats**
1/2 cup **bran**
pinch of **salt**
1/2 cup **pecan nuts**, chopped
2 tablespoons **soft dark**
  brown sugar
3/4 teaspoon **apple-pie spice**
6 tablespoons **butter**, melted

Put all of the prepared fruit and raisins into a
shallow, rectangular ovenproof dish, approximately
11 x 8 inches. Drizzle over the reserved pear juice.

Mix together the dry topping ingredients in a large
bowl. Pour over the melted butter and combine until the
mixture resembles large bread crumbs. Sprinkle over
the fruit and press down firmly.

Place in a preheated oven, 350°F, for 40–45 minutes
or until golden and crisp. Serve with fat-free plain
yogurt, if desired.

For forest fruit & clementine crumble, replace
the fresh and dried fruits with 3 cups frozen forest
fruits, thawed and drained of excess liquid. Slice
2 clementines into segments, discarding the pith, and
mix with the forest fruits. Spread the fruit over the base
of the ovenproof dish, cover with the crumble topping,
and bake as above.

very berry yogurt fool

Serves **4**
Preparation time **5 minutes**,
plus cooling and chilling
Cooking time **about
5 minutes**

3 tablespoons **crème de
cassis** or **spiced red fruit
cordial**
1½ cups **mixed frozen
berries**
2–4 tablespoons
confectioners' sugar,
to taste
2 cups **low-fat plain yogurt**
1 cup **low-fat blackcurrant
yogurt**
1 **vanilla bean**, split in half
lengthwise
toasted **slivered almonds**,
to serve (optional)

Put the crème de cassis or cordial in a saucepan over a low heat and gently heat, then add the berries. Stir, cover, and cook for about 5 minutes or until the fruit has thawed and is beginning to collapse. Remove from the heat and stir in 1–3 tablespoons of the confectioners' sugar, according to taste. Cool completely, then chill for at least 1 hour.

Mix together the plain and blackcurrant yogurts and 1 tablespoon of the confectioners' sugar in a bowl. Scrape in the seeds from the vanilla bean and beat to combine.

Fold the berries into the yogurt mixture until just combined. Carefully spoon into decorative glasses or glass serving dishes and serve immediately, sprinkled with toasted almonds, if desired.

For exotic fruit fool, replace the crème de cassis with 3 tablespoons coconut cream and the mixed berries with 1½ cups exotic fruit mix and add 1 tablespoon lime juice. Heat as above, then blend in a food processor or blender until smooth. Chill as above. Mix the plain yogurt with 2 tablespoons coconut cream and 1 cup fat-free mango yogurt instead of the blackcurrant yogurt. Fold in the fruit puree and serve sprinkled with toasted coconut flakes, if desired.

vanilla-spiced fruit salad

Serves **4**
Preparation time **10 minutes**, plus cooling
Cooking time **4–5 minutes**

²/₃ cup **apple juice**
1 **vanilla bean**, split in half lengthwise
2 tablespoons **agave nectar** or **light brown sugar**
2 **kiwi fruit**, peeled and sliced
1¼ cups hulled and thickly sliced **strawberries**
1 cup **blueberries**
1 **mango**, peeled, pitted, and sliced
mint leaves, to decorate

Warm the apple juice in a small saucepan with the split vanilla bean and agave nectar or sugar over a medium-low heat. Simmer gently for 4–5 minutes, then allow to cool completely. Remove the vanilla bean and scrape the seeds into the light syrup.

Combine the fruits in a large bowl and drizzle over the vanilla-spiced syrup. Stir gently to coat and spoon into serving bowls. Sprinkle with mint leaves and serve.

For Asian-style fruit salad, replace the apple juice with ²/₃ cup pineapple juice and simmer in a saucepan with 2 star anise, 1 tablespoon lime juice, 2 cloves, and the agave nectar. Allow to cool, then chill for 1 hour. Cut off the top and base of 1 small pineapple and slice off the skin. Cut the pineapple into quarters and remove the core from each quarter. Cut into slices and combine with the mango, a 13 oz can drained litchis and 2 sliced star fruits in a serving bowl. Pour over the syrup and serve.

apple & blackberry pie

Serves **4**

Preparation time **20 minutes**, plus chilling

Cooking time **35–40 minutes**

1¼ cups **whole-wheat flour**

¾ cup **all-purpose flour**

¼ lb (1 stick) **chilled butter**

1 tablespoon **superfine sugar**

pinch of **salt**

3 **dessert apples**, peeled, cored, and sliced

1 teaspoon **lemon juice**

1 teaspoon **almond extract**

1–2 tablespoons **dark brown sugar**, to taste (optional)

1½ cups **fresh** or **frozen blackberries**

2 tablespoons **toasted, chopped almonds** (optional)

Place the flours in a large bowl, add the butter, and blend in with the fingertips until the mixture resembles fine bread crumbs. Stir in the superfine sugar and salt. Mix in 3½–4½ tablespoons cold water, adding enough water to form a dough, and knead lightly until smooth. Divide into 2 balls, one slightly larger than the other. Wrap each in plastic wrap and chill for 30 minutes.

Put the apples, lemon juice, almond extract, and brown sugar in a bowl and toss to coat. Mix in the blackberries and set aside.

Roll out the larger ball of pastry on a lightly floured surface to fit a 9 inch nonstick pie pan. Press the pastry into the pan to come up the sides, moistening the edges with a little cold water. Roll out the smaller ball to fit as a lid. Spoon the fruit evenly over the pastry shell, then sprinkle with the almonds, if using. Top with the pastry lid, pressing down the dampened edges to seal. Trim away the excess pastry with a sharp knife.

Cut 3 small incisions in the top of the pie and place in a preheated oven, 350 °F, for 35–40 minutes or until crisp and golden. Allow to rest for 5–10 minutes, then serve in slices with low-fat sour cream.

For rhubarb & raspberry pie, replace the dessert apples with 4 cups thinly sliced rhubarb and the blackberries with 1½ cups fresh or frozen raspberries and add the freshly grated zest of 1 lemon. Bake as above until the pastry is crisp and the rhubarb tender. Stir 1 teaspoon rose water into 4 tablespoons low-fat sour cream and serve with the pie.

papaya with tumbling berries

Serves **4**

Preparation time **8 minutes**

2 large **papayas**
1 cup **blueberries**
1 cup **raspberries**
1¼ cups sliced **strawberries**
½ cup **cherries**, pitted
  (optional)
honey, to taste (optional)
lime wedges, to serve

Cut the papayas in half and scoop out the seeds and discard. Place each half on a serving plate.

Mix together the blueberries, raspberries, strawberries, and cherries, if using, in a bowl and then pile into the papaya halves. Drizzle with a little honey, if desired, and serve with the lime wedges.

For papaya & berry smoothie, peel and halve the papayas, remove the seeds, and cut into chunks. Place in a food processor or blender with the remaining fruits and 10 ice cubes. Add 2 cups apple or guava juice and blend until smooth. Pour into glasses and serve immediately.

balsamic strawberries & mango

Serves **4**

Preparation time **5 minutes**, plus overnight chilling and standing

3 cups **strawberries**, thickly sliced

1 large **mango**, peeled, pitted, and sliced

1–2 tablespoons **superfine sugar**, to taste

3 tablespoons **balsamic vinegar**

2 tablespoons chopped **mint**, to decorate

Mix together the strawberries and mango in a large, shallow bowl, sprinkle with the sugar, according to taste, and pour over the balsamic vinegar. Cover with plastic wrap and chill overnight.

Remove the fruit from the refrigerator and allow to stand for at least 1 hour before serving.

Spoon the fruit into serving bowls, drizzle over the syrup and serve, sprinkled with the mint.

For peppery strawberries & blueberries, mix the strawberries with 1 cup blueberries and make as above. Sprinkle with a few grinds of black pepper and the chopped mint before serving.

griddled bananas with blueberries

Serves **4**
Preparation time **5 minutes**
Cooking time **8–10 minutes**

4 **bananas**, unpeeled
8 tablespoons **fat-free plain yogurt**
4 tablespoons **steel-cut** or **fine rolled oats**
1 cup **blueberries**
honey, to serve

Heat a ridged griddle pan over a medium-hot heat, add the bananas and griddle for 8–10 minutes, or until the skins are beginning to blacken, turning occasionally.

Transfer the bananas to serving dishes and, using a sharp knife, cut open lengthwise. Spoon over the yogurt and sprinkle with the oats and blueberries. Serve immediately, drizzled with a little honey.

For oat, ginger, & golden raisin yogurt, mix ½ teaspoon ground ginger with the yogurt in a bowl. Sprinkle with 2–4 tablespoons dark brown sugar, according to taste, the oats and 4 tablespoons golden raisins. Allow to stand for 5 minutes before serving.

pear, almond, & chocolate cake

Serves **4**
Preparation time **10 minutes**
Cooking time **45–50 minutes**

6 tablespoons **peanut oil**
½ cup **fat-free plain yogurt**
1 teaspoon **vanilla extract**
¾ cup **golden superfine sugar**
2 cups **whole-wheat flour**
½ cup **ground almonds**
2 teaspoons **baking powder**
pinch of **salt**
3 **eggs**, lightly beaten
½ cup **bittersweet chocolate chips**
1 large firm, ripe **Comice pear**, peeled, cored, and coarsely grated
⅔ cup **whole blanched almonds** (optional)

Beat together the oil, yogurt, vanilla extract, sugar, flour, ground almonds, baking powder, and pinch of salt in a large bowl. Add the eggs, one by one, beating well after each addition.

Fold in the chocolate chips and pear and spoon into a deep, round 8 inch nonstick cake pan. Arrange the blanched almonds over the top of the cake, if using.

Place in a preheated oven, 350°F, for 45–50 minutes or until the cake is risen, golden, and firm to the touch.

Allow to cool for 15 minutes in the pan, then remove from the pan and cool completely on a wire rack. Serve in thick wedges with dollops of low-fat sour cream, if desired.

For lime & blueberry yogurt cake, make as above, replacing the vanilla extract with the grated zest of 1 lime and the pear with 1 cup blueberries. Omit the chocolate chips and blanched almonds. Sprinkle 2 tablespoons shredded coconut over the top before baking. Bake as above.

rice pudding with toasted nuts

Serves **4**
Preparation time **5 minutes**
Cooking time **35–30 minutes**

½ cup **brown pudding rice**
3 cups **skim** or **lowfat milk**
2 **cardamom pods**, lightly
  crushed
finely grated zest of ½ **lemon**
2 tablespoons **dark brown**
  sugar, plus extra to serve
  (optional)
1 **vanilla bean**, split in half
  lengthwise
¾ cup mixed blanched
  nuts, such as **Brazil nuts**,
  hazelnuts, and **shelled**
  pistachio nuts

Put the rice in a heavy saucepan with the milk, cardamom, lemon zest, and sugar. Scrape in the seeds from the vanilla bean and place over a medium heat. Bring to a boil, then reduce the heat, partially cover, and simmer very gently, stirring regularly, for 25–30 minutes, or until the rice is tender and creamy, adding more milk if necessary.

Meanwhile, place the nuts in a small freezer bag and tap lightly with a rolling pin until they are crushed but not ground. Tip into a nonstick skillet and dry-fry over a low heat for 5–6 minutes, stirring continuously, until golden. Tip onto a plate and allow to cool.

Spoon the rice pudding into deep bowls and sprinkle over a little extra brown sugar, if desired. Sprinkle with the toasted nuts and serve immediately.

For fresh fig compote, to serve as an accompaniment, put 4 roughly chopped fresh figs and ½ cup apple juice in a small pan and simmer gently for 10–12 minutes or until the fruit is tender. Either leave the compote chunky or blend to a puree in a food processor or blender.

creamy mango & passion fruit

Serves **4**
Preparation time **10 minutes**

1 large **mango**, peeled, pitted, and cut into chunks
3 cups **fat-free plain yogurt**
1–2 tablespoons **agave nectar**, to taste
1 **vanilla bean**, split in half lengthwise
4 **passion fruit**, halved

Place the mango in a food processor or blender and blend to a puree.

Put the yogurt and agave nectar, according to taste, in a large bowl, scrape in the seeds from the vanilla bean, and beat together. Gently fold in the mango puree and spoon into tall glasses or glass serving dishes.

Scoop the seeds from the passion fruit and spoon over the mango yogurt. Serve immediately with thin cookies, if desired.

For blackcurrant & almond yogurt, puree 2 cups black currants, as above, and fold into the yogurt with the agave nectar, according to taste, and 1 teaspoon almond extract. Spoon into tall, glass serving dishes and sprinkle with toasted almonds, to serve.

mixed berry salad

Serves **4–6**
Preparation time **10 minutes**

3 cups **strawberries**
2 cups **raspberries**
1½ cups **blueberries**
1 cup **blackberries**
1 small bunch of **mint**, finely chopped, a few sprigs reserved for decoration
3 tablespoons **elderflower syrup**

Hull and halve the strawberries. Wash all the berries and drain well.

Put the berries in a large serving bowl and add the chopped mint and elderflower syrup. Mix together carefully and serve, decorated with the reserved mint sprigs.

For warm berry salad, dilute 6 tablespoons elderflower syrup in 2½ cups water, add ¼ cup superfine sugar and bring to a boil in a heavy saucepan. Add the berries, prepared as above, to the pan and turn off the heat. Let the berries cool slightly, then serve with low-fat sour cream. The berries will keep for up to 5 days in the syrup in the refrigerator.

index

235

acknowledgments

Executive Editor: Eleanor Maxfield
Managing Editor: Clare Churly
Senior Art Editor: Juliette Norsworthy
Designer: Penny Stock
Photographer: William Shaw
Home Economist: Joy Skipper
Props Stylist: Liz Hippisley
Senior Production Controller: Caroline Alberti

Special photography: © Octopus Publishing Group Limited/William Shaw
Other photography: © Octopus Publishing Group Limited 75, 151; /Stephen Conroy 6, 13, 71, 140, 174, 208; /David Munns 32, 49, 62, 77, 81, 89, 117, 133, 161, 165; /Lis Parsons 14, 25, 65, 98, 109, 113, 121, 127, 139, 153, 169, 201, 203, 205, 233; /William Reavell 97; /William Shaw 69; /Ian Wallace 43, 57, 207.